THE CONSERVATIVE PARTY FROM
HEATH TO THATCHER

To my parents and to their grandchildren,
Jonathan and Mark

The Conservative Party from Heath to Thatcher

Policies and Politics 1974–1979

ROBERT BEHRENS
Lanchester Polytechnic

SAXON HOUSE

Published by

Saxon House, Teakfield Limited,
Westmead, Farnborough, Hants., England

British Library Cataloguing in Publication Data

Behrens, Robert
   The Conservative Party from Heath to Thatcher
   1. Conservative and Unionist Party — History
   2. Great Britain — Politics and government —
   1964.
   I. Title
   329.9'41   JN1129.C72

ISBN 0 566 00268 X

Printed in Great Britain by
Biddles Ltd, Guildford, Surrey

Contents

The Author

Robert Behrens is Lecturer in Public and Social Administration at Lanchester Polytechnic, Coventry. He was educated at Burnage Grammar School, Manchester, and at the Universities of Nottingham and Exeter. He has supported Manchester City F.C. since 1952.

Acknowledgements

R.E. Dowse read the whole manuscript and tried to impress upon me the importance of rigour and clarity in writing. (Fine teachers are not always blessed with good students.) Douglas Owen reviewed each chapter and made countless helpful suggestions. Iain Hampsher-Monk applied his customary perception to the problem of improving three chapters. Maurice Goldsmith, Bruce Coleman and Kevin Williams made valuable comments on individual chapters. Many Conservative politicians and officials found time to give me assistance, but none more than Tony Speller who disagreed with almost everything I wrote and still encouraged me to keep writing. Two of Lanchester's recent and astute graduates, Nick Irving and Peter Dixon, did efficient bibliographic work. John Irwin of Saxon House handled the project with speed and courtesy. Last, my parents bore the brunt of the occasional bad humour associated with writing a book, and more besides. I am indebted to all these people, but the inadequacies that follow are mine alone.

R.F.B.
Palmerston Lodge,
1 July 1979.

1 The character of Conservative politics

'Nurtured on the simple virtues of service and hard work, and deferent to the idea of political opportunity, Mrs Thatcher succeeded Mr Heath as Conservative leader in February 1975. From then on she was responsible for the spring in the step of anyone bred over a grocer's shop south of the River Trent, and a good many more to boot.'

In March 1974, little more than three years after winning a general election and embarking upon a silent 'revolution' to transform the face of British society, the Conservative party found itself in opposition. This was an uncomfortable position at the best of times, but since it had been precipitated through an early and unsuccessful call from a Conservative government for a vote of confidence from the British electorate, these were not the best of times. Faced with a Labour government which rivalled Gladstone and the Turkish Empire in its refusal to expire, the Conservative party remained in opposition until May 1979. Then, with a different leader and a changed outlook it was called upon by the electorate to undertake the responsibilities of office once again. This book is a study of the Conservative party between these elections. It is an attempt to make sense of the policy debates and personality clashes which occurred over five long and fretful years.

There were three principal characters in our history. The first was Mr Edward Heath, Conservative party leader from 1965 until 1975, and Prime Minister between 1970 and 1974. Born in Broadstairs, Kent, in 1916, one of Mr Heath's earliest recorded actions was to go out into his father's garden and pull up all the vegetables.[1] To many Conservative MPs this was a protentous act, since by 1975 they regarded Mr Heath as quite the most radical politician of his day, whose career was best summarised as a succession of root-pulling and unsettling gestures. In the wake of his exit from Downing Street, following a confrontation with the National Union of Mineworkers, Mr Heath manifested symptoms of severe shock (see chapter 3) and a year later after being removed as Conservative party leader he retired brooding to his tent. In the course of the following four years (see chapter 7) he reappeared from time to time, displaying in what Lewis Carroll might have called an agony in several fits, the various masks of architect

1

of national coalition, aggrieved former leader, man of conscience, scribe of the 1970 Government and, rarely, loyal party man. Very occasionally the authentic Edward Heath might have surfaced through it all, but as even his close political companions noted their inability to penetrate his inner thoughts, such intimacies were clearly not for the consumption of the public.[2]

Sharing the forefront of Conservative politics with Mr Heath were two politicians who decided in 1974 that they disputed his interpretation of true Conservatism. First, there was Sir Keith Joseph, a sensitive soul with a hesitant manner which his internalisation of the certainties of Hayek could do nothing to assuage. Sir Keith differed from Mr Heath in that he danced like a pixie on the grave of the 1970 Government (of which he was a senior member) as if the Constitutional Convention of Collective Cabinet Responsibility was but a twinkle in the eye of his father. Then there was Mrs Margaret Thatcher who played David to Sir Keith Joseph's Jonathan. Nurtured on the simple virtues of service and hard work, and deferent to the idea of political opportunity, Mrs Thatcher succeeded Mr Heath as Conservative leader in February 1975. From then on she was responsible for the spring in the step of anyone bred over a grocer's shop south of the River Trent, and a good many more to boot. As such she was the object of attention of countless biographers who poured over her native Grantham in search of trinkets from an ordinary past.[3] The extent to which Mrs Thatcher excited mental agitation can be gauged from the various characterisations of her as Iron Maiden, Wicked Witch of the Western World and Chief Recruiting Officer for the National Front. Not perhaps since Arthur Balfour won the epithets Niminy-Piminy, Lisping Hawthorn Bird and Brutal Bloody Balfour was a Conservative leader the object of such abuse. There were strong admirers too. Many of them sent letters to *The Daily Telegraph* to identify themselves, though none of them quite matched the fervour of Professor Denman who wrote from Pembroke College, Cambridge, to suggest that someone had better 'weave and work in wisdom the kerchief to dry from her (Mrs Thatcher's) eyes such tears as angels weep.'[4]

Occasionally other politicians burst upon the scene to snatch some of the limelight. Mr Michael Heseltine won a certain renown for his party conference rhetoric and his mace-waving in the House of Commons and Mr William Whitelaw occasionally appeared to make it absolutely plain what it was he was thinking. Last there was Mr Enoch Powell who seemed to make as little as possible absolutely plain. By February 1974 Mr Powell had come to haunt rather than tread the boards of Conservative politics. In the belief that Mr Heath's case for the February 1974 general election was fraudulent, and estranged by the loss of parliamentary sovereignty inherent in the

2

Conservative-led United Kingdom entry into the European Economic Community, Mr Powell stood down as the Conservative candidate in Wolverhampton South West. He did not seek election to Parliament again until the general election of October 1974, and then as an Ulster Unionist and not a Conservative. With his classical analogies, his obsession with what he called honour, his love of Parliament and his subordinate clauses, Mr Powell hovered like some latter-day Joseph Chamberlain (as he seemed to see himself) believing that in the face of the supreme constitutional issue of sovereignty, nation must come before party.

Each of these characters made some contribution to the history of the Conservative party after 1974, but the essence of what happened is not entirely related in the inter-play of personalities.[5] Other factors intervened to complicate matters. The first can be labelled 'the search for true Conservatism'. A problem for any political party is how to keep the power entrusted through victory at a general election, or how to regain power once it has been lost. Conservatives have attended to this problem by trying to find a satisfactory answer to the question 'What will you conserve?', and thereby coming to some conclusions about the nature of Conservatism. This has involved a variety of sentiments at different times. In the 1840s it meant conserving the Irish on rotten potatoes (protectionism); in the 1870s it meant beating up the Zulus (imperialism); and after 1885 it involved inciting the citizens of Belfast to overthrow the rule of law in the name of the conservation of the Kingdom (unionism). Whatever conclusions were reached, they were usually dressed up in the bunting of common sense. This was a shield against reason and intellect which between them had wrought havoc over Europe.[6]

When the Conservatives lost office in 1974 they too embarked upon a debate about what to conserve, and in chapter 2 it is suggested that this debate is best displayed by the use of the terms 'Diehard' and 'Ditcher'. The Diehards viewed post-war Conservatism as merely an alternative form of socialism. The problem was that Conservatives had deviated from the eternal principles of limited government, sound money and moral rectitude. Ditchers on the other hand were less cavalier in their condemnation of post-war experience, since to them circumstances governed principles and they judged that intervention by the state had been not only beneficial, but also unavoidable in a society determined not to return to inter-war maladies.

The chief purpose of the book is to display the debate between the Diehards and the Ditchers and to spell out the consequences when one of the groups was in the ascendance. Since these consequences embrace the possibility of change not just in policy, but in the way in which policy was made and in party organisation, some attention must be paid

3

to the environment in which the debate was conducted. Historically, certain attitudes and assumptions permeated Conservative politics to give a distinctive flavour to the way in which the debate was carried out. The most important of these was the belief that government as an activity was best attended to by strong and relatively unencumbered leadership.[7]

Conservative party leaders were therefore vested with a huge amount of formal authority embracing the making of policy, the control of the party's central bureaucracy (Conservative Central Office) and the appointment of the shadow cabinet when in opposition. The concomitant of wide leadership discretion was the existence of numerically important sections of Conservative politics consulted and even fêted, but consistently relieved of the arduous task of making what were seen to be 'political' decisions. For example, the annual conference of the National Union held out many opportunities including exposure to the media, assessing the mood of the faithful, kite flying and even socialising or swimming, but it rarely rose above the level of careful stage management.[8] Similarly, the local party associations were kept busily involved in fund raising and bringing out the vote on election day, activities important in themselves but removed from the subtleties of policy making at the national level.[9] Although Conservatives acquiesced in wide leadership authority, there were well defined limits to acquiescence. Conservative leaders had to be prepared to listen to their followers and be responsive to them. When they stepped outside this wide parameter they were reminded that the leader's job was leasehold rather than freehold, and they were called to account.[10] The average tenure of a Conservative leader between 1902 and 1975 was only about seven years which suggests, if nothing more, that the absence of formal mechanisms for the removal of the leader was not a hindrance to the aim of accountable leadership.

Without resorting to undue jargon we can call this view of leadership style and distribution of responsibilities within the party 'the traditional form of conversation' in Conservative politics. It is important to see the extent to which this traditional form held general approval after 1974 since its existence would have limited the amount of change envisaged when, for example, a Diehard replaced a Ditcher as leader of the party. It is clear that the traditional form of conversation did exist after 1974, and that this helped to rule out certain fundamental changes in the character of the Conservative party.

The form of our study is conceptual rather than chronological. In chapter 2 the debate about what Conservatives thought worth conserving is examined. In chapter 3 the 1975 leadership election is subjected to scrutiny and the way that Conservative views about authority told against Mr Heath is illustrated. Chapter 4 contrasts the leadership of Mrs Thatcher with the leadership of Mr Heath. The differences in style are highlighted but it is argued that in terms of policy formation and organisation the Conservative party remained substantially unchanged, in large part because both leaderships were committed to major aspects of the traditional form of conversation in Conservative politics. In chapters 5 and 6 the important areas of economic policy and industrial relations are examined. The tensions between Diehard and Ditcher prescriptions are displayed, and official party policy under Mrs Thatcher is contrasted with policy under Mr Heath. In these chapters and in chapter 7 the continuity in policy across the Heath and Thatcher eras is demonstrated and juxtaposed with the expectations of change evinced by the ascendance of a Diehard leader and the enunciation of Diehard sentiments. One of the conclusions to be drawn from this continuity (it is suggested in chapter 7) is that Mr Heath's dissent after 1974 cannot be explained solely in policy terms. In chapter 8 some general conclusions are drawn about the extent of change that the Conservative party experienced after 1974. Change was limited by the consensus over the form of conversation in Conservative politics, by the existence of a consensus between Diehards and Ditchers in some policy fields and by the caution of Mrs Thatcher's Diehard leadership. However, in some important respects the party did change significantly. The unusual circumspection which ruled after 1975, though an impediment to policy change, did in itself represent something of a new departure from the ethos that had governed Conservative politics since 1965. Furthermore, the party became dominated by a leadership which was fervent in its articulation of non-interventionist sentiments and critical of the contemporary record of the Conservative party. The consequences this had for the attractiveness of the Conservative appeal in the 1979 general election, for the standing of the Constitutional Convention of Collective Cabinet Responsibility and for the place of honour in Conservative politics are all discussed.

The historical approach used in this study has been criticised by political scientists as '. . . pernicious and disruptive in the study of politics . . .' since it encourages, even justifies '. . . armchair constructions of what must be the case.'[11] While there is no attempt here to apply the rules of scientific method to Conservative politics, the charge of armchair speculation is in this case rejected entirely. In the search for information the author has, literally, immersed himself in Conservative politics. This means more than 'monitoring' *The Daily Telegraph* over toast and marmalade. Conservative politicians and officials have been sought at their work, at their clubs, at their conferences, in the Houses of Parliament and on the stump. From Bideford to Bradford the search for understanding has continued, by courtesy of British Rail and through the goodwill of busy politicians. The limitation of the study is not so much armchair speculation, but that the reduction and therefore elevation of a large number of past events into a smaller body of significant material has been a subjective exercise. If subjectivity of this kind had not constrained even learned historians this writer might well have expressed contrition: but as it did,[12] he does not.

Notes

1   Heath, 'Home Town', *The Sunday Times Magazine*, 1 February 1976.
2   Interview with Heath minister, 6 April 1977; Walker, *The Ascent of Britain*, 1977, p.59; Maudling, *Memoirs*, 1978, pp 142, 206.
3   Murray, *Margaret Thatcher*, 1978; Gardiner, *Margaret Thatcher from Childhood to Leadership*, 1975.
4   Denman, letters, *The Daily Telegraph*, 18 February 1976.
5   Young, *Victorian England: Portrait of an Age* (1953), 1969, p.174.
6   Disraeli, *Coningsby or the New Generation* (1844), 1967, p.199; Wellington, quoted in Longford, *Wellington: Pillar of State* (1972), 1975, p.258; Balfour, quoted in Dugdale, *Arthur James Balfour*, 1936, 11, pp 404-5; Baldwin, quoted in Butler, *The Art of the Possible: the Memoirs of Lord Butler* (1971), 1973, pp 16-17.
7   Beer, *Modern British Politics* (1965), 1969, p.92; Glickman, 'The Toryness of English Conservatism', *Journal of British Studies*, 1962, pp 131-2; Raison, *Why Conservative?*, 1964, p.30; Disraeli, op.cit., p.200.
8   McKenzie, *British Political Parties* (1964), 1967, p.189; Rose, *The Problem of Party Government*, 1974, p.142.
9   Rose, op.cit., p.156; Bulpitt, 'English Local Politics: the Collapse of the Ancien Régime?', *PSA Conference Paper*, March 1976.
10   McKenzie, op.cit., pp 62-145; Beer, op.cit., p.246.
11   Stanyer, 'Irresistible Forces: the Pressures for a Science of Politics', *Political Studies*, 1976, p.242.
12   Carr, *What is History?* (1961), 1972, pp 1-24; Elton, *The Practice of History* (1967) 1976, pp 82-6.

2 The Diehards and Ditchers

'. . . it is very difficult to find any conservatives at all in the Conservative party. Mr Edward Heath with his problem solving approach and his reorganization of central government, Sir Keith Joseph with his crash course in Hayek, Friedman and Toqueville, and Lord Hailsham with his new-made written constitution, were actors on the same, not different plane. They were rationalist men incarnate, dabbling in the politics of in-experience and behaving — to follow Oakeshott's analogy — like jumped-up kitchen porters confusing the art of cookery with the activity of reading cookery books.'

This chapter attempts to give a coherent description and analysis of the divisions in Conservative politics after 1974. It argues that the most illuminating distinction is between Diehard and Ditcher. Diehards argued that since the Second World War Conservatives had abandoned their fundamental principles and donned collectivist clothes. Political power and national well being could only be regained if Conservatives set aside such collectivism and died hard on limited government, individual freedom and moral rectitude. Ditchers on the other hand maintained that consistency could be more a vice than a virtue, since policies must be changed (or ditched) in the light of changing circum-stances. The chapter also attempts to show the important consensus stretching across political ends and means that Diehards and Ditchers shared. In defending the use of the terms Diehard and Ditcher against alternative juxtapositions such as left and right or conservative and rationalist, attention is drawn to the unconservative flavour of con-temporary Conservative politics.

To give order to the search for true Conservatism by dividing the Conservative party up into neat and coherent groups is in part to dis-tort it. While we may fairly split the party into Diehards and Ditchers there are several complicating factors. First, Diehard and Ditcher are blanket and artificial terms covering a wide variety of policy views. Diehard, for example, embraces those who saw themselves as populists, radical rightists, the new right, libertarians, whigs, young men in a hurry, media men and sociology baiters. It represents a continuum ranging from what was ill informed prejudice dressed up as commonsense at one end, to high intellectual endeavour at the other. What delineates the Diehards is their basic assumption that the postwar settlement[1] had failed because of the overweening interference of the state in society. This belief had ramifications which tended to push the Diehards along the same prescriptive path towards less state spending and therefore more 'freedom' and responsibility. It would be sensible however not to underestimate the diversity within the category. Certainly there was no institutional unity, since Diehards were located in such various bodies as the Selsdon Group, the National Association for Freedom, the Institute of Economic Affairs and the Centre for Policy Studies. The second complicating factor is that some Diehards only emerged in 1974. In the 1950s and 1960s, and in Mr Heath's administration after 1972, they defended and built on the postwar settlement, which after 1974 they began to denigrate. Judged therefore by their record in government they were Ditchers, but on the strength of their intent they were Diehards.

The Ditchers were united in their belief that postwar interventionism, for all its faults, was based on the principles essential for a sound body politic. The term Ditcher embraces Keynesians, Butskellites, growthmen, anti-growthmen, managerialists with ardour cooled by experience, young men in not quite such a hurry, Heathmen, anti-Heathmen and Tory reformers. Some Ditchers were by political principle out of experience. Keen to join with Mr Heath in implementing his 'silent revolution' in 1970, experience in government had taught them the merit of balance over consistency, and making the best of policy reversals in 1971 and 1972, they embraced the Ditcher cause.

The Diehard road to freedom

Diehard analysis began with a condemnation of postwar state activity. Sir Keith Joseph, for example, exclaimed in June 1974 that for a generation, in their competitive attempts to improve living standards, politicians had overestimated the power of government to manipulate the economy and change society. This interventionism, manifest in the form of high taxation, universal welfare, centralised planning, state control and spending, had led to three decades of debilitation.[2] The pursuit of three fashionable ideas had precipitated disaster. The first was a concern for social justice which assumed that society rather than native wit and intelligence was responsible for relative differences in wealth and living standards. The corollary of this idea was that the

8

state should act to remedy inequalities, and in doing so it had concentrated on social welfare at the expense of its defence obligations. For Mr Robert Moss therefore — echoing Professor Hayek — the idea of social justice was a grave threat to civilisation.[3] The search for the middle ground had been equally damaging. According to Sir Keith Joseph it was nothing more than the lowest common denominator reached by splitting the difference between the Conservative and ever more extremist Labour position.[4] The middle ground was therefore a slippery slope to socialism and to Dr Rhodes Boyson only a euphemism for appeasement.[5] It certainly took no account of popular feeling. The third concept in vogue was the idea of national continuity, which Mr Angus Maude contended encouraged Conservatives to consolidate the Labour-inspired drift towards egalitarianism, permissiveness and the steadily increasing power of the trade unions. As a result citizens believed that they were no longer effectively represented in politics.[6]

The key to Diehard prescriptions for this malaise lay in their respect for the market mechanism. To Mrs Thatcher the market was a democracy in which people could cast their vote every day as they went about their business making decisions about how to spend their own money.[7] To Sir Keith Joseph, eyes freshly raised from Hayek's *The Road to Serfdom*, it was a device enabling talented people to pursue careers beholden only to consumers rather than placemen.[8] The genius of the market economy stemmed from the interaction of supply and demand, which acted as a self regulating mechanism encouraging efficiency and innovation, distributing labour and increasing choice. Private enterprise, Mrs Thatcher assured an American audience, was therefore by far the best method of harnessing the energy and ambition of the individual to increase the wealth of the nation.[9]

Confidence in market forces structured Diehard thought over vast areas of public policy. The key tasks were seen to be to reduce the role of the state in society, to divorce politics both from economics and from social policy, and to banish monopoly from the private sector. Thus, for example, the state was to be shunted from the area of wages policy and from the activity of funding inefficient industry; the welfare state was to be more fully exposed to the curative waters of competition from the private sector; and in industrial relations, trade union monopolies of labour, which distorted supply and demand, were to be abolished or at least regulated. In these circumstances the role of the state would be minimal. There was general agreement that it should control internal law and order and external defence, that it should attend to preventive public health, provide limited social services, and certain public services like roads and street lighting. Diehards also agreed that the state should undertake a minimum regulation of the economy to ensure competition by breaking up monopoly, and to cushion social change by provision of regional policy, unemployment benefit and retraining schemes.

While the rigour of the market was important for Diehards, they argued that a necessary concomitant was a return to personal responsibility. Moral regeneration was required to transform the meaning of freedom from licence into restraint. Addressing Edgbaston Conservatives in 1974, Sir Keith Joseph argued that family, and what he called civilised values, the foundation on which the nation was built, were being undermined. Socialism was to blame because it took responsibility away from families, divesting parents of their duty to provide for family security, health and education. This was disastrous because when responsibility was taken away from people they became irresponsible. The result was that while standards of living had risen, crime was on the increase, illiteracy was rife, and educational standards were in decline.[10] The task to be undertaken, Sir Keith later told the Economic Research Council, was to recreate conditions for 'the forward march of embourgeoisement, which went so far in Victorian times'. An important element in bourgeois values was deferred gratification, the ability 'to work hard for years, study, save, look after the family future'. It also involved self discipline and an aversion from instinct and spontaneity. However, in the postwar world, a 'pop culture' which indulged licence, and inflation, which promoted spending rather than saving, had discouraged this march. As crime and violence had less to do with poverty than with the erosion of bourgeois values, the reinstatement of those values would be salutary.[11] Some Diehards came to similar conclusions but for slightly different reasons. To populists in Conservative politics, like Mr Teddy Taylor, it wasn't so much that bourgeois values were good in themselves but that working class citizens believed that they were. The populists thought that the duty of the Conservative party was to 'leap across the class barrier' and reflect the concerns and views of ordinary citizens on issues which were of immediate concern to them. Amongst the most salient issues were housing, education, crime and immigration.[12]

What is curious about Diehard thought is that its intellectual forebears, Hayek and Friedman, resist the title 'Conservative'. Hayek, for example, suggests that Disraeli is the kind of writer likely to appeal to totalitarians, and condemns Conservatism for having no substantive ideals.[13] In this sense it is clearly to be differentiated from his own liberal creed. Such eclectic ancestry helps us to understand three features common to Diehard analysis. The first was a reverence for nineteenth century liberal ideas and experience. Sir Keith Joseph, for example, warned an Oxford audience in March 1975 not to be deterred 'by sneers of those who consider that any idea which is more than a couple of decades old is bad by definition, unless it was written by

Marx or Lenin'.[14] In similar vein, Dr Rhodes Boyson saw the Victorian period as a golden era of economic expansion, advance in personal satisfaction and charitable provision, which stood in sharp contrast to contemporary socialist stagnation.[15] The second feature was a new Conservative deference for the Liberal politician, Gladstone, as a champion of retrenchment and limited government. Dubbed by his Conservative opponents as so impulsive and excitable that he had to be regarded as a kind of lunatic,[16] Gladstone re-emerged in the Diehard liturgy as one who never forgot the supremacy of the moral over the expedient. Evidently, Disraeli's belief that posterity would do justice to that 'unprincipled maniac' was misplaced. The third feature is that contemporary Conservatives began to talk a good deal about 'the free society', as if it were to be located just south of the Selsdon Park Hotel. The ramifications of this are interesting. How, for example, should one interpret Dr Boyson's most explicit attempt to delineate the free society? His blueprint borrowed so much from Victorian experience that his radical programme outlined in *Centre Forward* can be seen as a device for overcoming Professor Hayek's reservations about the lack of substantive content in Conservatism. However, an alternative conclusion to be drawn is that all Dr Boyson succeeded in doing was to turn Conservatism into liberalism. In the most amusing account of political history this century, George Dangerfield wrote of *The Strange Death of Liberal England*. Perhaps the destiny of the contemporary observer of Conservative politics is to be the historian of life after death.

Two further observations about the Diehard analysis seem appropriate. First, politicians who exhorted individuals to assume once again responsibility for their economic and social actions were clearly under certain reciprocal constraints. To carry conviction, these politicians were obliged to make themselves equally responsible for their own political decisions. How far some Diehard politicians met this obligation as members of the Heath administration which so heartily embraced the postwar settlement is open to doubt, and is discussed in chapters 7 and 8. Second, in *The Road to Serfdom*, Professor Hayek argued that socialists deployed the epistemological trick of portraying power as freedom to make the idea palatable.[17] Armed with such an excellent precedent, the student of politics has good cause to consider carefully what Diehards meant when they talked and wrote about freedom and the free society. Dr Boyson, for example, in waxing lyrical about the free society in *Centre Forward*, observed that it was doubtful whether strikes by firemen, ambulancemen and prison workers should be allowed. He further suggested that, as long as state nationalised monopolies were allowed to continue, the prohibition of strikes was the least compensation the public could be offered for lack of choice in

11

these areas. Given that such proposals were coupled with a questioning of the necessity of picketing, it is not unreasonable to conclude that at least one Diehard's interpretation of freedom was somewhat equivocal in meaning.[18]

Ditchers and Disraeli

To the Ditchers, Diehard concentrations on the merit of liberal thought were irritating and bizarre. In the first place, the conditions under which liberalism had thrived no longer existed. British success in the free trade era had rested on military and political power to exploit competition-free markets. Now, however, both the power and the markets had disappeared.[19] Second, liberalism argued that once the rules of market theory were allowed to operate, the well ordered society from which they were derived could be restored. This meant, Mr William Waldegrave suggested, that Diehards had nothing to say to public sector workers or protectionist trade unionists except that the world would be a better place if only they did not exist.[20] Liberalism concentrated on market theory, but the external world of social facts and realities carried on in spite of it. The third problem with liberalism was said to be that it had to rest on moral foundations. Liberal premises about freedom were conditioned by ideas of moral rectitude, deference and restraint. Yet, because in the postwar world of spontaneity and licence such values had become dissipated, the task for the Diehard was, in Sir Keith Joseph's phrase, to 'remoralise whole groups and classes of people'. By this activity, Ditchers suggested, the Diehards were encouraged to abandon the very trust in individual preferences which they regarded as important. In addition, as Mr Reginald Maudling explained, Diehards gave the impression that they favoured a return to suppression. This was inappropriate given that conventions about behaviour changed with succeeding generations.[21]

To confront Diehard charges of lack of fidelity to principle, Ditchers championed the idea of circumstances, and rather than attack the postwar settlement, they defended it. After 1974 Ditchers were to be found sulking in their tents, enjoying long luncheons at Wiltons, lounging on the backbenches in the House of Commons, translated (somewhat abruptly) to the House of Lords, and writing — if not reading — Tory Reform Group pamphlets. Ditchers accepted that mistakes had been made in the last thirty years — state provision of welfare had gone too far, politics had been over concerned with managerialism and had neglected ideals — but they denied that the Conservative party had strayed from its true course. They defended the operation of the postwar settlement on the grounds that it flowed naturally from war time Conservative thinking, and that it was the only viable strategy to secure the twin aims of renewed Conservative electoral success and a potentially healthy body politic.

To the Ditchers, it was fanciful to suppose that the Conservative party committed to a Diehard programme in the postwar period could have won popular support. Conservatives had been blamed by the electorate for the interwar unemployment, and as Sir Ian Gilmour explained, to rid themselves of this stigma they were obliged to acquiesce in the greater role for the state prescribed by Keynes to relieve unemployment.[22] The alternative was electoral ruin, and Mr Peter Walker warned that unless Conservatives ensured that the state in capitalist society showed social responsibility of this kind in the future, they would never be able to win mass support.[23]

How was the second aim of a sound body politic made more likely by the operation of the postwar settlement? Ditchers argued that the true Conservative role was to create or maintain a sense of community in society. This could be achieved by winning the loyalty of the people to the state, an activity accelerated by the use of the majesty of state apparatus as a balancing force in society. Winning the allegiance of citizens was a vital process and loyalty would not be deep unless the state provided material protection and benefit. Loyalty was certainly not engendered by what one Ditcher called 'Homilies to cherish competition and warnings against interference with market forces'.[24] It was more likely to derive from the use of political skills to create a fresh equilibrium between different elements and doctrines in society when their imbalance threatened social harmony. This, Mr Heath explained, was the historic role of the Conservative Party.[25] It legitimised, for example, scepticism in the face of pure monetary theory and apparent inconsistency in the face of changed circumstances. The Conservative party would act now to restrict the influence of unwieldy union power and now to instil caution where capitalism sank to exploitation.[26] In times of undue individualism the party might defend the state, yet in times of state authority and socialism, it would champion the individual.[27] Confronted with the question 'What will you conserve?', the Ditcher response was an unabashed, 'That depends'.

The logic of the need to foster a sense of community, therefore, was that the Conservative party must use the state on the scale inherent in the postwar settlement. It had to ensure that social and political considerations superseded market forces to safeguard jobs, safety and health. State activity of this kind was likely to be extensive because the Ditchers had no great faith in the ability of the market mechanism to engineer equitable solutions. Rather, they agreed with Mr Peter Walker that it condemned the weak and was a powerful source of social disorder.[28] What followed was that under Conservative direction the state could not stand aside, but must intervene to promote, for example, a creative partnership with industry and unions.[29] Furthermore, the Conservative party could certainly not afford to be merely the stern and unbending defender of bourgeois interests. It had to be the party of effective social reform.[30]

Two observations can be made about Ditcher faith in equilibrium, community and state intervention. First, it led to the use of symbolism markedly different from that deployed by Diehards. For example, rather than condemn the middle way in politics as a road to socialism, Ditchers venerated it as a compromise between reaction and revolution.[31] It offered a secure foundation on which to base policies urgently required to solve Britain's economic and social problems.[32] In addition, because of their distrust of liberalism, Ditchers gave nothing like the deference given to Victorian England by Diehards. To the Ditchers, Victorians were naive in their belief that Britain was permanently fixed upon a course of progress, and harsh in the tough penal codes they adopted. Not surprisingly, therefore, Gladstone was relegated from his position as godfather of principled politics and dressed again in the familiar garb of incessant moraliser and base fellow. Disraeli not Gladstone was the prophet.

The Ditcher use of Disraeli as a legitimiser for their operation of the postwar settlement was founded on a highly selective account of his long career and reference to edited highlights of some of his early novels. His patchy record of support for social reform was subordinated beneath a recollection of extravagant phrases drawn from *Coningsby* and *Sybil* lauding the 'social happiness of the millions', the continuity of institutions and authoritative leadership.[33] The possibility that these exquisite felicities of style had more to do with being beastly to Peel than with practical social policy was never considered. Instead, summoned from his nineteenth century grave, Disraeli became doyen of national and patriotic policies, scourge of the unacceptable face of capitalism, champion of the working classes and social reform and watchdog of the constitution. For the Ditchers indeed, Disraeli rivalled Katie in what he managed to do, and supported everything in the postwar world with the possible exception of Manchester City.[34] The second observation is that the notion of balance was certainly attractive to those who saw political activity as being literally an aimless exercise with neither starting point nor appointed destination. However, it was also a refuge for political idealists who, having set out in their salad days (and after) for an appointed destination, realised that they could not reach it. In 1970, for example (see chapter 3) a great deal was heard from Mr Heath and his colleagues about the need for certain specific managerial reforms and policies to be instituted, and rather less

14

about the need for scepticism and balance in British politics. Many of these prominent Ditchers embraced the weaponry of certain parts of Ditcher analysis somewhat late in the day.

While Diehards and Ditchers argued about the important question of the role of the state, there was a considerable degree of consensus between them about the aims of Conservative political activity, the propriety of devices to achieve these aims and the manner of conversation in Conservative politics. Both groups, for example, expressed a keen faith in the importance of wealth and property. The Ditcher, Mr Robert (later Lord) Carr wrote that the widespread ownership of property was an essential guarantee of personal liberty and independence from the state. It was also a defence against radical ideologies, since 'sensible' people (those with property) would have an interest in continuity. To a Diehard like Mrs Thatcher, this was all commonsense. In her opinion a Conservative reluctant to consider private property as one of the bastions of individual freedom was not really worthy of the name and was effectively lost to socialism.[35] The consensus about the tools of political activity embraced the importance of growth which most Ditchers and Diehards thought desirable since it was an instrument to improve social welfare and might conceivably add to the quality of life.[36] There was also agreement on the necessity of upholding the rule of law and the constitution. When the Ditcher Lord Hailsham wrote in *The Door Wherein I Went* that the doctrine of liberty under the law was the 'golden thread' which alone gave meaning to the political history of the West, he distanced himself from Diehards like Mrs Thatcher only in the graciousness of his prose. Freedom under the law honoured human dignity, Mrs Thatcher explained to an American audience in 1975, and provided an economic opportunity to bring prosperity.[37] Last, agreement about the manner of conversation in Conservative politics stemmed from shared views about authoritative leadership and the importance of original sin. To the Ditcher Mr Heath, for instance, Conservatives feared disruption of the orderly development of society because man was more imbued with original sin than with noble savagery.[38] In similar vein, the Diehard Dr Boyson concluded that man was still tribal, bearing in mind the postwar fragmentation (sic) of Africa and the behaviour of many football crowds. The job of the Conservative party, he asserted, was to channel these feelings and contain them.[39] Such gloomy views about the unreason of man legitimised authoritative leadership, and conditioned Diehard and Ditcher agreement that the Conservative party should be run on a hierarchical basis. Both resisted what was called the democratisation of Conservative politics. This is borne in mind in chapter 4 when Mrs Thatcher's claim to have 'changed everything' after becoming party leader is critically examined.

Of course the Labour party had no interest in displaying this consensus. On the contrary, Labour politicians did their utmost to highlight the tensions between Diehard and Ditcher thought, particularly after the Conservatives embraced a Diehard leadership in 1975. No one was more adept at this than Mr Michael Foot, as he demonstrated in the House of Commons on the night his Government finally expired. Mr Callagham followed his example in the 1979 general election campaign itself, by claiming in Coventry that the Diehards had turned their backs on Disraeli in their determination to bring back 'privilege for the few and cold comfort for the many'. Other socialists contrived to be deliberately hazy in their distinction between general Diehard aspirations and specific Conservative party pledges. This allowed them to indulge in what Mr Angus Maude called 'a constant stream of lies' during the election campaign.[40]

It is important at this point to emphasise the modesty of the claims for a Ditcher/Diehard axis, which is neither an all embracing division taking in the range of policies debated by Conservatives, nor a classification including all Conservative politicians. With regard to European and foreign policy, for example, the epithet Diehard is at best likely to give only a hint about what policy view a politician endorsed. That Diehard thought was conscious of the debilitation of the nation engendered by the postwar settlement, certainly induced some Diehards to be sympathetic to arguments which claimed that the European Economic Community eroded Britain's nationality and British patriotism. However, other Diehards thought nothing of the sort and rallied quiescently to the European cause. Secondly, many Conservatives, especially in the parliamentary party, came into neither Diehard nor Ditcher category. For some of these, true Conservatism was really atavism in disguise, while others agreed with Mr William Whitelaw that 'what is best for our country and all its people should come first'.[41] This was so nebulous a definition that it came close to saying that Conservatism is 'what I say it is', and is perhaps best understood as having been loyalty to persons. The third point is that, like all ideology, while Diehard and Ditcher thought connected generalised beliefs with more specific opinions, there was room for controversy about what this thought meant in terms of immediate tactics and programme.[42] So, for example, in 1975 devolution was legitimised in the Diehard rosary as placing power back with the people where it belonged, while a year later it was banished on the grounds that it created more government and bureaucracy (see chapter 7). The transcendent nature of ideological statements did not remove judgement from Conservative politics and meant, for example, that in common with all politicians, Diehards could bend with the wind and keep a firm eye on the opinion polls.

Whatever the caution and limitation surrounding the division into Diehard and Ditcher, it is clearly appropriate in comparison to alternative dichotomies. The claims for a conservative and rationalist, a Conservative and Tory or a left and right classification are founded on unsuitability or on simplicity and confusion. To begin with, Professor Oakeshott's division between the conservative and rationalist disposition is unsuitable, even though it is one of the most thought provoking distinctions in political analysis. Oakeshott's conservative disposition is rooted in an acceptance of the current condition of human circumstances, which men have learned to enjoy and to manage. It involves a preference for the tried to the untried and for the near to the distant. For the conservative, government is the mundane activity of constructing general rules of procedure and providing redress to those who suffer from others behaving in a contrary manner.[43] Appropriate political action should be based on 'intimations' from tradition, which is a flow of sympathy containing an understanding of how to amend existing arrangements.[44] The rationalist, on the other hand, sees the conduct of affairs as a matter of solving problems and believes that no man can be successful if he surrenders his reason to habit or tradition. For him there is no problem which does not have a 'rational' solution, and the remedy for any particular problem is universal in its application. The rationalist sees only one kind of knowledge, that to be learned from a book. He relies on written doctrine rather than traditional behaviour. Doctrine, however, is an abstraction and therefore a distortion of traditions of behaviour. Because it contains only half of experience the doctrine of the rationalist will make him at least always half wrong.[45]

Now the problem with this division is that it is very difficult to find any conservatives at all in the Conservative party (or any other party). Mr Edward Heath with his problem solving approach and his reorganisation of central government, Sir Keith Joseph with his crash course in Hayek, Friedman and Toqueville, and Lord Hailsham with his new-made written constitution,[46] were actors on the same, not different plane. They were rationalist men incarnate, dabbling in the politics of inexperience and behaving — to follow Oakeshott's analogy — like jumped-up kitchen porters confusing the art of cookery with the activity of reading cookery books. When therefore the Ditcher Sir Ian Gilmour conjured up textual references from Oakeshott to build up his case against the doctrine of the Diehard guru Hayek, we can reasonably assert that this was an activity similar to the arsonist who urged a colleague in the criminal classes to imbibe Dicey's strictures on the rule of law.[47] In summary, Oakeshott offers a clear distinction but not one which distinguishes between contemporary Conservative politicians. Why should their political disposition have been so unconservative?

Perhaps because the politics of inexperience is founded on a lack of confidence about how to handle political developments. The decline of the aristocratic element in the Conservative party leadership, the increasing concern at national economic decline and the collapse of Conservative electoral fortune under Mr Heath (three defeats in four general elections) all contributed to the mood of uncertainty conducive to rationalist politics after 1974.[48]

A second possible classification is to distinguish between Conservative and Tory. This creates more problems than it solves. The term Tory is used to signify different meanings. First, it is a shorthand, journalistic expression to refer to all members of the Conservative party. It is also a pejorative term used by emotional politicians like Aneurin Bevan, Lloyd George and Sir Harold Wilson to refer to the privileged backgrounds of their political opponents. Third, the word Tory is used to label beliefs which favour a strong, authoritative leadership, concerned for the condition of the people and the continuity of institutions. Dissenting movements within Conservative politics are often dressed as 'Tory' in this third sense to add legitimacy to a cause which is then contrasted with an opportunistic and unprincipled official Conservatism. Toryism therefore becomes the articulation of dissident ideas, a ready weapon in the hands of Disraeli, Lord Randolph Churchill and Mr Enoch Powell in their rebel days. Disraeli, as an opponent of Peel's leadership, for instance, wrote that Conservatism was a bad thing, treating institutions like pheasants: preserving them for no other purpose than destruction when the clamour went up against them. However, when the rebels rejoin the official line (Mr Powell excepted) Conservatism is magically restored to its integrity, becomes a 'good thing', and thus indistinguishable from Toryism. To add to the confusion, those who have not been rebels argue all along that Conservative and Tory principles are one and the same thing. This is a quicksand better left to the leader writers of *The Daily Star*.

The third possible classification involves a distinction between left and right. The left wing of the party confronts the right wing in what might be called the politics of association football. The popularity of this approach has been such that two texts, a thoughtful and learned one by Sir Ian Gilmour, and a bold cavalry charge by Dr Rhodes Boyson, have been saddled with the respective titles *Inside Right* and *Centre Forward*. There are, however, several problems about this classification. First, the concept of a 'wing' adorns Conservative politics with a suggested unity about policy choices which it does not deserve. The right wing, for example, has been both for and against the Common Market, for and against a statutory incomes policy, and for and against the restoration of capital punishment. This is because it is a hotch potch of groups with libertarian, authoritarian, paternalistic and

18

nationalistic sympathies, which dissolves into fragments at the first hint of scrutiny. Second, the left/right split masks the shift of policy choices in the political spectrum. Thus, while monetarism, public expenditure cuts, balanced budgets and free collective bargaining were right wing in 1965, a decade later they were acquiesced in by many of those described as left wing. The mania for universality in the labelling of political opinion has invested dialogue and disputation in British politics with a rigidity which it does not obviously deserve. Third, the dichotomy underestimates the underlying consensus about certain fundamentals. Political aims (wealth and property) appropriate means (growth and law) and the traditional manner of conversation severely constrained the disputation in the party. The bitterness of the quarrel among Conservatives after 1974 should not be permitted to hide the fact that politicans were conducting warfare on a limited ground and according to agreed rules. Last, and crucially, the politics of association football dictate that the residue of Conservatives, those neither left nor right, is centrist. This is a nonsense for it is simply in equilibrium. After 1974 the residue was engaged in a variety of activities or states of exis-tence: resting — probably at Prunier — being atavistic, or adjusting loyalties to fit the change in party leadership. None of these activities or states of being was a guarantee of moderation, whatever that was. The student of politics should not be conned into believing that a Con-servative politician sitting in the House of Commons with his eyes closed was necessarily dreaming of the middle way or the political genius of R.A. Butler. The honourable member might simply have been asleep.

Notes

1   See Gamble, *The Conservative Nation*, 1974, p.29: part of this chapter appeared as 'Diehards and Ditchers in contemporary Conserva-tive Politics', *The Political Quarterly*, 1979.
2   Joseph, *Reversing the Trend*, 1975, p.7.
3   Moss, 'Defence of Freedom', *In Defence of Freedom*, 1978, pp 141-4.
4   Joseph, *Stranded on the Middle Ground?*, 1976, pp 19-26.
5   Boyson (ed.), *1985: An Escape from Orwell's 1984*, 1975, Intro-duction.
6   Maude MP, letters, *The Times*, 7 May 1974.
7   Thatcher, Glasgow, quoted in *Conservative Monthly News*, Summer 1978.
8   Joseph, 'Interventionism in Britain', *Crossbow*, Summer 1978.
9   Thatcher, 'Let the Children Grow Tall', *Margaret Thatcher in*

North America: Extracts from the Leader's Speeches . . . September 1975, ND, p.9.

10   Joseph, quoted in *The Daily Telegraph*, 21 October 1974.

11   Joseph, 15 January 1975, *Reversing the Trend*, 1975, pp 56-7.

12   Interview with Conservative MP, 15 February 1978.

13   Hayek, *The Road to Serfdom* (1944), 1976, p.160; Hayek, *The Constitution of Liberty*, 1960, pp 397-8.

14   Joseph, 14 March 1975, *Reversing the Trend*, 1975, p.72.

15   Boyson, *Centre Forward*, 1978, p.128.

16   Cranbrook, quoted in Cooke and Vincent, *The Governing Passion: Cabinet Government and Party Politics in Britain, 1885-6*, 1974, p.66.

17   Hayek, op.cit., pp 18-19.

18   Boyson, op.cit., pp 43, 47-8.

19   Waldegrave, *The Binding of Leviathan*, 1978, pp 38-9.

20   Ibid., pp 39, 60.

21   Joseph, quoted in *The Daily Telegraph*, 21 October 1974; Maudling, 'Questions Tories Must Answer Before Seeking Change at the Top', *The Times*, 3 February 1975.

22   Gilmour, *Inside Right*, 1977, pp 19-20.

23   Walker, *The Ascent of Britain*, 1977, p.28.

24   Gilmour, op.cit., p.118.

25   Heath, 'My Kind of Tory Party', *The Daily Telegraph*, 3 February 1975.

26   Waldegrave, op.cit., p.45.

27   Gilmour, op.cit., pp 103, 148.

28   Carr, 'My Kind of Tory Party', *The Daily Telegraph*, 29 January 1975; Walker, quoted in *The Guardian*, 28 June 1978.

29   Walker, op.cit., 1977, pp 98-101.

30   Scott, 'Policies for Tomorrow', *The Cambridge Reformer*, October 1977, p.4.

31   Chairman, Tory Reform Group, quoted in *The Times*, 5 January 1976.

32   Walker, op.cit., 1977, pp 36, 39.

33   Disraeli, *Sybil or the Two Nations* (1845), 1927, p.339.

34   The confession by Disraeli that 'Certainly Manchester is the most wonderful city of modern times!' doubtless left Ditchers inclined to suspend judgement on even this last exception (*Coningsby or the New Generation* (1844), 1967, p.131); Waldegrave, op.cit., pp 49, 52; Gilmour, op.cit., pp 70-86; Walker, op.cit., p.35.

35   Carr, 'My Kind of Tory Party', *The Daily Telegraph*, 29 January 1975; Thatcher, 'My Kind of Tory Party', ibid., 30 January 1975.

36   Walker, op.cit., p.20; Joseph, op.cit., pp 36-7.

37   Hailsham, *The Door Wherein I Went*, 1975, pp 94-5; *Margaret Thatcher in North America: Extracts from the Leader's Speeches . . .*

September 1975, ND, p.16.

38   Heath, 'My Kind of Tory Party', *The Daily Telegraph*, 3 February 1975.

39   Boyson, op.cit., p.154.

40   Foot, *Hansard*, 28 March 1979, col.575-84; Callaghan, quoted in *The Financial Times*, 25 April 1979; Maude, quoted in CRD, *Daily Notes*, 27 April 1979, p.11.

41   Whitelaw, *CPC Monthly Report*, November 1974.

42   Dowse and Hughes, *Political Sociology*, 1972, pp 243, 256.

43   Oakeshott, 'On Being Conservative', *Rationalism in Politics*, 1962, pp 169, 186, 189.

44   Oakeshott, 'Political Education', *Rationalism in Politics*, pp 123-4, 126.

45   Oakeshott, 'Rationalism in Politics', *Rationalism in Politics*, 1962, pp 4-5, 11, 22, 30-31.

46   Hailsham, *The Dilemma of Democracy: Diagnosis and Prescription*, 1978.

47   Oakeshott, op.cit., p.22; Gilmour, op.cit., p.115.

48   Butler and Sloman (eds), *British Political Facts, 1900-1975*, 1975; Whitelaw, *CPC Monthly Report*, August/September 1974; Biffen, *A Nation in Doubt*, 1976, p.5.

3 The election of Mrs Thatcher

'The majority of Conservative MPs were affected in a slightly less prodigious way. Like maiden aunts taking the waters at Eastbourne, they inhaled sharply, held their noses and submerged for a count of ten. The leadership election, Conservatives believed, was a necessary evil, something to be got through rather than enjoyed. The sooner the whole distasteful business could be concluded the better'.

This chapter examines the contest to elect a Conservative leader which took place in February 1975. Several aspects of this contest are examined. First the timing of the election is discussed. Why didn't the leadership election take place immediately following the February 1974 general election defeat? It is shown that while there was pressure on Mr Heath to resign in the spring of 1974, this was prevented by the lack of an institutional device to test the leader, and by the fear that a contest would precipitate another general election. Diehards and Ditchers nevertheless used the period between March 1974 and February 1975 to rehearse the leadership election by jockeying for position and articulating their respective interpretations of true Conservatism. Second, the procedure adopted for the leadership election is assessed. It is argued that this took its coherence (or more pertinently its incoherence) from Conservative views about authority. Third, the substantive content of the election campaign is scrutinised. In discussing the criticisms of Mr Heath and the election of Mrs Thatcher, it is argued that Mr Heath's leadership style — which was *in part* at variance with the traditional form of conversation in Conservative politics — offended more than just Diehard opinion. In consequence, although the election of Mrs Thatcher represented a Diehard triumph, it was also a vote in favour of a return to the traditional style of authoritative Conservative leadership. We speculate on the extent to which it was equally a vote expressing dissatisfaction at the party's recent electoral record.

There was undoubtedly a feeling in the party after the February reverse that Mr Heath's leadership should at least be subject to confirmation. Some made no secret of their view that Mr Heath should resign and, in a rather vitriolic editorial, *The Spectator* described Mr Heath as a 'squalid nuisance' as leader who had spent 'nine years trying to ruin the Conservative Party . . .'.[1] More important, there was disquiet in the parliamentary party, and it is likely that as many as 100 Conservative MPs told the Conservative whips that they could not win another general election with Mr Heath as leader.[2]

As soon as Parliament met, the Conservatives had to decide whether or not to try and defeat the new Labour Government in the House of Commons. By combining with all the other opposition parties the Conservatives could defeat the Government, but most probably at the cost of a general election, because Mr Heath's unsuccessful attempt to form a coalition with the Liberals in March demonstrated the lack of an alternative to the Labour Government in the new Parliament. Few Conservatives felt optimistic about the possibility of winning a general election so soon after the February defeat. Most thought it would have meant the Labour Government going to the polls with the advantages of having no record to defend, of possibly being able to accuse the Conservatives of irresponsibly precipitating an election, and with the three-day week still fresh in the public mind.[3]

To this delicate situation the Conservatives brought tired and shell-shocked minds. They were tired because the Conservative ministers, particularly Mr Heath, had endured a period of severe physical strain while in office, especially in the last two months, and once displaced from government a reaction set in. As one member of the Heath Government explained, 'It was only when we stopped that we realised how tired we were'.[4] They were shell-shocked because they had expected to win the election, and the defeat was what Mr Timothy Raison described as 'the greatest shock to the party since 1945'.[5] The combined effect of these two states of mind probably adversely affected judgements for some time. For example, after having promised to behave as a responsible opposition, the shadow cabinet promptly tabled an amendment to the Queen's Speech which, if supported by the minor parties, would have brought the Government down within weeks of gaining office. Confronted with forty dissidents threatening abstention, at the last moment, the shadow cabinet decided not to force a vote.

In the wake of this ineptitude, a number of backbenchers went to the chairman of the 1922 Committee, Mr du Cann, to demand an election for the leadership. Mr Heath was advised by Lord Hailsham to 'sit tight' and did so.[6] In terms of the prolongation of his leadership in the short term, this was probably sensible advice for there were two factors which militated against any immediate threat. First, the rules for the election of leader, introduced in 1965, contained no provision for subjecting the incumbent leader's position to confirmation. New rules would therefore have to be devised (at the instigation of the leader only) and this followed by a contest, was bound to be time consuming, divisive and potentially traumatic for the party. Conservatives feared (and this was the second reason) that no sooner had they embarked on such a process than the Prime Minister, Mr (later Sir Harold) Wilson, would seek an early dissolution of Parliament to capitalise on the uncertainty and division in the opposition camp. Many Conservatives therefore felt that while to fight with Mr Heath as uncontested leader might mean certain defeat at the next election, it would be less disastrous than fighting an election as a party whose leadership was being formally tested.[7] For the moment then, Mr Heath remained.

Subsequent Conservative tactics were more circumspect. The shadow cabinet settled on the idea of giving qualified support to some Labour measures (notably the second reading of the Finance Bill) and of concentrating on winning arguments rather than votes.[8] This involved ensuring that the Conservatives never voted at full strength, or what the Liberals called thundering then funking. Complaints were made at the 1922 Committee that these were farcical tactics,[9] and even those who saw no alternative were depressed by the constraints of the situation. As one shadow minister explained, 'It was all rather frustrating. We wanted to defeat the Government but knew that if we did it might be electorally disastrous'.[10] The end of the 'phoney' war was called in the middle of June, by which time the intervention of the holiday period ensured that no election could be called until late September. Between June and September therefore, aided by the minor parties, the Conservatives imposed 18 defeats on the Government in the House of Commons, and important amendments were made to Labour legislation. In such circumstances morale began to pick up in the parliamentary party, and Mr Heath's own spirit also revived. In part this was due to the warm welcome he had received on a visit to China where one of his friends commented, 'Mao was the first person he had seen in months who was actually pleased to see him'; but it was also because Mr Heath began to think that there might be a chance of winning the next election.[11]

After February, the Conservatives had to decide whether their general election rebuttal was an indication from the voters that their Ditcher policies were unacceptable, or whether it could be attributed to the unexpected and damaging incidents of the campaign (the Figgures row and the Adamson 'faux pas'[12]) and the electorate's tardiness in recognising the supposed merit of the Conservative position. Between

24

March and September 1974, a shadow cabinet steering committee, a series of policy groups chaired by shadow ministers, and the Conservative research department debated and thought through what Mr (later Sir) Ian Gilmour called this 'acute dilemma'.[13] While Lord Carrington called for a review of the whole of Conservative economic and industrial policy, in the shadow cabinet only Sir Keith Joseph, with some support from Mrs Thatcher and Sir Geoffrey Howe, believed that Diehard prescriptions were required. The majority of the shadow cabinet acquiesced in the view of the Ditcher Mr Ian Gilmour that there was scant temptation for the Conservatives to change course in the election to come. This attitude was implicit in Mr Heath's refusal to appoint an economic affairs review group which would have been dominated by Diehards from the parliamentary party's finance committee.[14] Whatever the majority in the shadow cabinet thought however, the Diehards were not prepared to let the matter rest. In their political manoeuvrings and in the Ditcher responses to them between March and October 1974, lay the origins of the suspicion and bitterness which was to sour the leadership election and subsequent relations in the party.

In the wake of the general election defeat, Sir Keith Joseph had gone to Mr Heath to say that he did not want a specific shadow responsibility. He suggested that it would be useful to be free to examine the experience of other industrial nations, particularly West Germany, to see what lessons could be learned.[15] The Conservative shadow chancellor, Mr Carr, acquiesced in this proposal with the proviso that he and Sir Keith worked in some kind of unison. Sir Keith apparently agreed. Against this background the Centre for Policy Studies emerged, sponsored by Sir Keith Joseph and Mrs Thatcher. The declared aim of the centre was to 'secure fuller understanding of the methods available to improve the standard of living, the quality of life and the freedom of choice of the British people, with particular attention to social market policies'. It was intended that it should operate one step back from policy to work on changing the climate of opinion in which policy was developed. In this sense it was alleged not to be a rival to the Conservative research department which concentrated on producing immediate policy briefs.[16]

If there was any expectation that such a new venture could be launched without controversy, it was quickly dispelled. Ditcher suspicion of the centre arose from a misunderstanding about its purpose and from the independent manner of its operation. First, after Sir Keith Joseph's conversation with Mr Heath, Ditchers in the shadow cabinet believed that the centre would confine its scope to foreign economies and they were taken aback when it began to give Diehard briefings on the British economic situation. This may help to explain why Mr Heath later claimed that the centre was set up without his knowledge, even though it was established that he had nominated Mr Adam Ridley, one of his economic advisers, to the centre's management committee.[17] Second, the Ditchers became angry when money was collected for the CPS at a time when the Conservative research department was run down, short of money, and able to provide almost no help to shadow spokesmen on economic matters. Leading Ditchers in the shadow cabinet met to discuss this situation, and one recalled that 'Anyone else but (Sir) Keith and we would have been suspicious. But he was seen to be the least ambitious member of the shadow cabinet'.[18]

At the end of August 1974, when the shadow chancellor was on holiday, Sir Keith Joseph announced to his colleagues that he planned to make a major speech in Preston, questioning the validity of the approach of the last Conservative government. For the first time proceedings became acrimonious, and despite protestations, Sir Keith declined to make major alterations to his text. He had already given some public intimation of his re-think at Upminster in June, but at Preston on 5 September Sir Keith spelled out in detail his conversion to liberal economics and the Diehard cause. Inflation, he asserted, was a self inflicted wound. It had been primarily the result not of world prices increasing, but of postwar governments creating new money out of proportion to the additional goods and services available. This ended in deficit financing which was disastrous, because any effective control of inflation had to be based not on a statutory control of prices and incomes but on maintaining the overall balance between the growth rate of money being spent and the growth of production. If this made him a monetarist, then Sir Keith said he acquiesced in the description. Inflationary pressure had been created by successive governments because politicians were haunted by the fear of long term mass unemployment, and had too often expanded demand as a panacea for what was really a whole variety of types of unemployment, which were not susceptible to such a remedy. The problems of temporary or of fraudulent unemployment and 'unemployables', for example, were not responsive to the expansion of demand, so all that was achieved was increased unemployment. 'What we have to do', Sir Keith said, '. . . is to set a level of domestic demand sufficient for that level of full employment which can be sustained without inflationary pressures . . . ' and then to work within it to attack specific employment problems. This would entail additional unemployment, but failure to take these steps would lead to worse unemployment later.[19]

The Diehard response to Sir Keith Joseph's speech involved a commotion and rejoicing rarely seen since the relief of Mafeking. The Ditchers, however, were not amused. They believed that Sir Keith had been disloyal in disassociating himself from official Conservative policy

26

so near to a general election, and that he had done the Conservative party a disservice by associating it in the public mind with increased unemployment. Furthermore, they were angry with him for not debating the matter in shadow cabinet, where it was asserted that he had stayed silent for most of the time, interjecting only when economic policy discussion had been concluded. Diehards retorted that Sir Keith had specifically explained in his speech that he was not saying that a certain level of unemployment was needed to avoid inflation, and that he had been forced into a public utterance by the failure of the shadow cabinet to give him a proper hearing.[20]

While there was no fundamental repudiation of the 1970 Government record, the Conservative leadership did amend their policies in three respects to try and win back their national constituency at the coming election. First, future industrial policy was to be marked by an attitude of conciliation hardly contemplated in February. Notably, the Conservatives pledged not to reintroduce the Industrial Relations Act rather than amend it, and they modified their bald February election broadcast threat to cut off benefits to strikers. Second, efforts were made to emphasise the desirability of returning to a voluntary incomes policy, with a statutory policy to be used only as a last resort. Third, new interventionist policies were produced to further the 'Conservative ideal' (sic) of a property owning democracy. These included a pledge to limit mortgage interest rates to 9½ per cent, and considerable help for first time house buyers and those who wished to buy their own council homes.[21] The details of the proposals were modified in shadow cabinet, but it is interesting that their inspiration derived from policy groups chaired by Mrs Thatcher who within a matter of weeks was to be heralded as an opponent of interventionism.

Alongside the modification of policy the Conservatives played the coalition card in the general election called for October. Until February 1974 Mr Heath had dismissed the need for a coalition,[22] but encouraged first by the iron hand of necessity in the form of an inconclusive general election result, and then by the sympathy for the idea manifest in certain sections of the party, he slowly turned towards it. In May, he charged Mr Douglas Hurd with the task of examining the psephological aspects of the problem, in June he began to talk of a 'programme of national unity', and in August the matter was discussed in shadow cabinet.[23]

The publication of the Conservative manifesto *Putting Britain First* gave the first indication that the national unity theme might have an institutional dimension, but this was clouded in ambiguity. The Conservatives would seek a majority in the election but use it to 'consult and confer with the leaders of other parties and with the leaders of the great interests in the nation'.[24] This Delphic utterance was forced on

27

the Conservatives because it was not clear who would be responsive to the initiative. The Labour party saw a coalition as 'the greatest "con" trick ever', and the possibility of any kind of alliance with the Liberals was much reduced by the equivocal attitude of extra-parliamentary Liberal officials towards an entente with the Conservatives. This took the wind out of the coalition kite flying of Mr Thorpe and Mr Steel. There was also the question of Mr Heath's leadership. Many Liberals and not a few Conservatives saw this as a stumbling block to any inter-party alliance. While Mr Heath discussed with close colleagues the possibility of stepping down, he decided against such a course. There remained the possibility that seasoned men from outside politics would be brought in, but here also Mr Heath remained vague and refused to name names. This uncertainty about the composition of a government of national unity carried with it a concomitant vagueness about the kinds of policies it would propose, and Mr Heath certainly made no attempt to outline a minimum programme of action. The government by Marks and Spencer remained firmly under wraps.[25] It was not until the weekend before polling (which took place on 10 October) in his final message to Conservative candidates that Mr Heath explicitly committed the party to the idea that 'a National Coalition government involving all the parties could be formed'. It was a decision taken without reference to the shadow cabinet which did not meet once during the campaign. Mr Heath declared that when the Conservatives obtained a majority he would set out to establish a government that could transcend party divisions.[26] The fourth reverse for the Conservatives in five general elections relieved him of the opportunity of trying.

The passing of the October election and Mr Heath's unsuccessful attempt to play the coalition card, provided the Conservatives with the opportunity to bring his leadership to account. Partisans could no longer argue that the threat of an imminent election made embarking on such an activity an unwise course, and there was not time enough to devise rules for a contest. There was wide agreement that an election should take place and public calls for Mr Heath's resignation came from Mr John Cordle, Mr Nicholas Winterton, and Mr Neil Marten who was reported as believing that the majority of Conservative MPs favoured Mr Heath resigning. Lord Hailsham thought such sentiment 'distasteful' considering that Conservatives had just campaigned for Mr Heath to be leader of a national government.[27] In addition to the public statements, the lobbying of the 1922 executive went on apace, with executive members being urged by Conservative MPs to take prompt steps to ensure that Mr Heath's position was given due consideration. The 1922 executive met on 14 October 1974 at Mr du Cann's Lord North Street home (the meeting had been arranged before the election) and were unanimous that a leadership election had to be held in the foreseeable future. This message was conveyed to Mr Heath who refused to play ball. He believed that the executive had no right to speak for the parliamentary party until 1922 elections had been held, and he wrote that he would discuss the situation with the executive after their re-election.[28]

The behaviour of the executive incensed supporters of Mr Heath. In the view of one Ditcher shadow minister, the executive had behaved improperly by stretching their tenure beyond a general election, and by striking at Mr Heath while grievances against him were at their highest. This action, he believed, had to some extent to be seen in terms of the long standing inability of Mr Heath and Mr du Cann to get on with each other. While Mr du Cann's public statements were those of a disinterested servant of the party, Ditchers considered that his political actions were those of a Diehard conspirator. The historian and joint secretary of the 1922 Committee wrote to *The Times* on 22 October 1974 defending the propriety of the actions of the executive. If good feelings still remained, their prolongation was not assisted when, on 15 October, the 1922 executive met in what they supposed was the quiet sanctuary of the Milk Street Offices of Keyser Ullman (the bank then chaired by Mr du Cann) to hear Mr Heath's reply. The press had been tipped off, and executive members were photographed leaving the premises. To members of the executive, the presence of the press was evidence of a 'dirty trick' perpetrated by supporters of Mr Heath. To Mr Heath's supporters however, the Milk Street incident was further proof of a sinister Diehard cabal operating from within the 1922 executive against Mr Heath.

During the rest of October, Mr Heath was the recipient of varying advice from his friends and allies on the merits and demerits of resigning and submitting himself to re-election. Further pressure emerged at the end of the month when at the first post election meeting of the 1922 Committee only two of more than twenty members who spoke came out in favour of Mr Heath. At this meeting Mr Kenneth Lewis pointed out that the party leadership was 'leasehold' rather than 'freehold'. Given that, in addition, on 7 November, the chairman and executive of the 1922 Committee were re-elected en bloc, Mr Heath's grasp of the leadership looked rather tenuous. In the face of all this pressure, in mid-November Mr Heath acknowledged himself to be 'the servant of the party', and he set up a committee under Lord Home to review the leadership election rules.[29]

The leadership election procedure

The Home proposals were accepted by Mr Heath and acquiesced in by all sections of the party, though few regarded them as satisfactory. This was not surprising since, although lacking a sanity clause, *The Procedure for the Selection of the Leader of the Conservative Party* was a complicated document which read at times as though it was a contract drawn up by Groucho Marx. There were four basic criticisms of it. First, as it involved three ballots, each with different rules, it was said to be too complicated. Second, it was said by Sir John Rodgers to be a 'cowards charter' because candidates were permitted to enter on the second ballot without having contested the first. Third, the 1975 rules provided for an annual election for the leadership, and made it more difficult than under the 1965 rules for a candidate (i.e. Mr Heath) to win on the first ballot. While in 1965 it was necessary on the first ballot to obtain an overall majority plus just 15 per cent more votes than any other candidate, this was altered in 1975 to an overall majority plus a lead of 42 or 15 per cent of *all* those entitled to vote. This was a small but significant raising of the hurdle, and led to suggestions that the rules were 'Alec's revenge' on Mr Heath for having succeeded him as leader in 1965. Lord Home dismissed these suggestions as 'perfectly ridiculous'. Fourth, while the National Union was given a consultative role in the procedure, it was denied any representation in the electoral college to choose the leader. This caused some resentment.[30]

Some Conservatives, including Lord Hailsham and Lord Home, later maintained that the old, so called customary process of consultation leading to the emergence of a leader, was a more satisfactory way of proceeding. The system had operated up to 1965 by party managers and prominent peers sounding out all sections of the Conservative party so that a new leader could emerge by general consent. The argument in favour of this process was that it was more democratic because it included the extra parliamentary party in the consultations, that it promoted unity, and that it added to the leader's authority and mystique. The idea that the customary process was more democratic is very dubious. Three examples illustrate this. In the first place, for the system to operate smoothly, Conservatives had to be very good at counting which was not always the case. In 1963 for instance, when the members of the Conservative cabinet were asked to indicate who should succeed Mr Macmillan (as party leader and therefore as Prime Minister) both Mr Iain Macleod and Mr Enoch Powell counted eight cabinet members in favour of Mr Butler, whereas agents for Mr Macmillan could only find two or three.[31] Next, the weight given to the opinion of each section of the party was determined arbitrarily by the party managers, with most bias usually given to the view of the leadership team. What would have happened in 1975, for example, when the majority of the parliamentary party opposed Mr Heath, yet the shadow cabinet opted strongly first for Mr Heath and then for

Mr William Whitelaw? It is certainly highly questionable whether Mrs Thatcher would have emerged if there had been no election. Third, the customary process left open the possibility of manipulation in the party hierarchy. Mr Macmillan's manoeuvres in 1963 were perhaps illustrative of this. By announcing that the customary soundings would begin while he was still Prime Minister, Mr Macmillan made it almost obligatory for the Queen to ask his advice. As his position was that almost anyone but Mr Butler should emerge, it can be argued that Mr Macmillan was taking every precaution to ensure that Mr Butler would not succeed him.[32]

There is not much evidence either that the customary process was especially efficient at promoting party unity. The fact that it worked reasonably well before 1975 owed more to the existence of natural successors to the leadership than to the curative balm of customary process. When there was no natural successor in 1963, the ensuant jamboree at the annual conference of the National Union at Blackpool left sections of the party convinced that injustice had been done. It so scarred Lord Hailsham's emotions that he confessed in *The Door Wherein I Went* that he was no longer able to write poetry, and it left an impression in many minds that the Conservative party had behaved in a ludicrous manner and was bereft of unity. It is not therefore easy to see why the customary process should have regained some popularity in 1975, unless one centres on the fact that it was an institutional device for articulating views about authoritative leadership. These views pushed certain Conservatives back into a world where men were either chaps, fellows or bounders, and quite away from what they regarded as the nausea of one man one vote by secret ballot. The majority of Conservative MPs were affected in a slightly less prodigious way. Like maiden aunts taking the waters at Eastbourne, they inhaled sharply, held their noses and submerged for a count of ten. The leadership election for them was a necessary evil, something to be got through rather than enjoyed. The sooner the whole distasteful business could be concluded the better. And if that meant putting up with a few bizarre and imperfect electoral rules, it was a small price to pay.[33]

Criticisms of Mr Heath

'Instead of being cold and wary, as was commonly supposed, he was impulsive and even inclined to rashness.' When he was 'reserved, tortuous, it was that . . . he did not see his way'. When he embraced new ideas 'he did so with eagerness and often with precipitancy . . . He was by nature very shy, but forced early into eminent positions, he had formed an artificial manner, haughtily stiff or exuberantly bland.'

31

His enunciation though clear was 'marred by provincialisms'. In some ways this is a fair summary of many of the criticisms weighed against Mr Heath, though in fact it was written of Sir Robert Peel by Benjamin Disraeli.[34] There were three major criticisms made of Mr Heath. The first concerned his leadership style and the way he had exercised his authority. To begin with he was said to be the rudest political leader since Andrew Bonar Law. However, Bonar Law at least insulted his opponents, whereas Mr Heath was alleged to be insensitive to and unfriendly with his own Conservative followers. Back in the halcyon days of 1970, one Conservative MP recalled, a great deal of resentment had already built up against Mr Heath because people were snubbed and their advice was ignored. When electoral fortunes turned sour this insensitivity took on a new importance. No Conservative appeared immune from the effects of Mr Heath's chilly disposition. Younger members complained of not being acknowledged in the House, senior backbenchers were dealt with in a high-handed fashion, and loyal colleagues treated with a curt incivility. Even dedicated Heath supporters compared Mr Heath's visits to the House of Commons smoking room with an inspection of the troops by the commander-in-chief. The result, as one prominent member noted, was that 'Edward has few friends, very few friends. If he falls down there will be nobody to pick him up'.[35]

In addition there was broad agreement that Mr Heath's leadership teams were unbalanced. It was suggested that after 1970 Mr Heath surrounded himself with like minded colleagues and that his cabinets and shadow cabinets were unrepresentative of the broad spectrum of Conservative opinion. The Diehard Mr John Biffen, for example, dryly observed after the construction of Mr Heath's last shadow cabinet, that the Conservative leader seemed to have been devoting more time to the scriptures as he had come up with the strategy of forming the shadow cabinet in his own image.[36] Last, there was a feeling that under Mr Heath too much power had accrued to the centre of Conservative politics, and that Mr Heath had tried to suppress those elements in the party whose views deviated from his own. While this complaint was generally articulated by Diehards, it ruffled Ditcher feathers too, and made Conservatives who acquiesced in Mr Heath's Ditcher policies somewhat reluctant to support him. Many grievances centred around the use of Conservative Central Office. Officially Central Office is the personal office of the party leader, but historically it has not taken on the character of an organisation geared to the personal interest of the leader. Its job has been to guide, inspire and co-ordinate the work of the party throughout the country without encroaching on the autonomy of the local associations in the selection of their candidates and agents, or on the running of their own organisations.[37] Mr Heath appeared to make Central Office more of the leader's personal machine than it had been previously. While Conservative leaders have tended not to make personal appointees party chairman, Mr Heath appointed a succession of his followers to the post after removing Mr du Cann in 1967. These included Mr (later Lord) Barber, Mr Thomas, Lord Carrington and Mr Whitelaw. In 1974 Mr Heath also made Mr Michael Wolff, a personal political adviser, director-general of Central Office, and responsible for co-ordination normally carried out by a career official. There was a feeling that as Central Office became more identified with the leader, it was used as a mechanism for disciplining and suppressing Mr Heath's opponents within the party. Mr Enoch Powell, for example, complained bitterly that Mr Heath suppressed every shade of difference and style right through from cabinet to constituency. According to Mr Hugh Fraser the result was a total domination of the party by one man.[38] Three instances of discipline and suppression caused particular concern. One involved the pressure placed on local parties to encourage their members to adopt pro-European attitudes during the passage of the Common Market legislation through Parliament. Mr Neil Marten, Mr Richard Body and Mr Ronald Bell were said to have been especially pressured, and some Diehard Conservatives concluded that Central Office was behind attempts to deprive them of the party nomination in the February 1974 general election.[39] Another instance of suppression involved the standing advisory committee on candidates which was more rigorous in vetting candidates for the February 1974 general election than it had ever been before. While since 1945, hardly any selected candidate had been denied official endorsement, in February 1974 three candidates were refused backing. Each of these was a Monday Club member, and a fourth, the Diehard Mr Alan Clark, faced Central Office obstruction until 1972. The third instance concerned the announcement in 1973 by the party chairman, Lord Carrington, of plans to make agents employees of the party at the centre rather than of constituency associations. While this had merit in terms of efficiency — it was the rich associations with comfortable majorities that could afford to attract the best agents — it also meant that agents might have transferred their first loyalty to Central Office and away from the locality. There was disquiet in the party at this measure of centralisation, and some saw it as an instrument to combat dissidence.[40] In summary, there appeared to be widespread disapprobation in the Conservative party that Mr Heath's conception of leadership placed too much emphasis on central control and too little on personal responsiveness. This can reasonably be interpreted as a manifestation of the desire to return to something closer to the traditional form of conversation in Conservative politics.

The second major criticism of Mr Heath's leadership came from those who believed that between 1970 and 1974, he was head of a government which abandoned Conservative principles. While the charge of desertion of principles was at the core of Diehard arguments, it was attractive outside the Diehard camp as well. This was because, in 1970, Mr Heath had shown none of the reticence or scepticism associated with Ditcher thought and had laid down in very specific terms what he saw his task to be. When, within two years of government, Mr Heath and his colleagues appeared to have dramatically changed direction, the memory of the bold promises remained. Apart from being exposed to Diehard onslaughts therefore, Mr Heath was also hoist by his own petard.

The thoughts of the Conservative leadership in 1970 were heavily influenced by what was seen as the instant politics and expediency of the 1966 Labour Government, and also by the problem solving emphasis of management thought. As a result, they saw politics not as the hazardous art of adjusting to changing and unpredictable circumstances, but rather as the ability not to be deflected from their course. The 1970 election manifesto, *A Better Tomorrow*, put the matter clearly when it stated that once a decision was made, once a policy was established, the Prime Minister and his colleagues should have the courage to stick to it.[41] The consequence of this perception of political activity was that the Conservatives made a large number of specific promises at the Selsdon Park conference, in their manifesto, and at their annual conference at Blackpool in October 1970. The manifesto confidently asserted that the aim was to replace Labour's restrictions with Conservative incentive, and that 'We utterly reject the philosophy of compulsory wage control'. It also rejected socialist intervention which usurped the function of management, sought to dictate prices and earnings in industry and which undermined self-reliance and initiative. In future, in the cause of profitability the Government would not, in the words of Mr John Davies, 'bolster or bail out' companies that could not be profitable. They would stop further nationalisation and, according to Mr Heath, the Conservative aim would be to bring citizens to recognise that they must be responsible for their own actions and certainly not expect the Government to step in and rescue them.[42]

While the Conservatives took action on a large number of their specific pledges, the Government deviated from the principal proposals it put before the electorate to such an extent that Mr John Biffen was driven to the use of Munich analogies to inquire if the 1970 manifesto was a mere scrap of paper. Three specific instances of betrayal were cited. The first was what Mr Enoch Powell described as the dispassionate acceptance of socialist solutions to emerging problems. He cited the nationalisation of Rolls-Royce as an example, and others referred to the abandonment of the non-interventionist industrial policy instanced by the decision to bolster and bail out the Upper Clyde shipyards, and the passing of the 1972 Industry Act. To Sir Frederick Corfield, himself a member of the 1970 government, all this was a puzzling way to demonstrate a belief in private enterprise.[43] The second alleged instance of betrayal was the adoption of a statutory policy for the control of wages and prices which, Mr Powell maintained, ministers had been unanimously repudiating until a few weeks before. The result of what the Diehard Mr Hugh Fraser called this growing tendency in the Conservative party to adopt a more collectivist outlook was, he maintained, that Conservative principles were falling by the wayside. The third instance of betrayal was said to be the decision taken, without the full hearted consent of Parliament and people, to join the EEC. To a small number of Conservative MPs this was contrary to Conservative principles because it was not part of 'Tory' faith to take evolving institutions and liberties and merge them with eight other nations into a new made state.[44]

The most vociferous and sustained attack came from Mr Enoch Powell who charged Mr Heath with deserting Conservative principles. Mr Powell had been estranged from the Conservative leadership since at least 1968, when he was dismissed from the shadow cabinet, and had been attacking the official Conservative lines on and off ever since. According to Lord Hailsham, Mr Powell's attacks on Mr Heath verged on the insane, and he was dubbed a fanatic by Mr Barber on behalf of the collective leadership at the 1973 annual conference. Mr Powell returned the compliment by publicly entertaining fears for the mental and emotional stability of Mr Heath in November 1973. What Mr Powell considered to be the Conservative leadership's ratting on the 1970 promises and principles, and his belief that the general election called by Mr Heath was essentially fraudulent caused him not to seek re-election as a Conservative MP in February 1974.[45]

The third major criticism of Mr Heath was that under his direction the Conservative party had fought four general elections and won a majority of seats once only. What made matters poignant was that many Conservatives saw a close relationship between this electoral failure and Mr Heath's own personality. It was said that he could excite the enthusiasm of neither the electorate nor of his own party workers. Mr Neil Marten put the problem about the electorate succinctly when he confessed that practically every MP he had spoken to had been confronted on the doorstep while canvassing in October with the sentiment 'I would vote Conservative but not as long as Mr Heath is there'. This Mr Marten said he thought unfortunate, but at the end of the day the Conservatives had to win the election. Mr Heath's inability to inspire his own party workers was also commented upon. Miss Joan Quennell, for example, wrote that, unlike previous leaders of the party

(Neville Chamberlain excepted) Mr Heath did not enjoy the warm and sympathetic support of the party's grass roots. Instead he had respect. Such a criticism was important in a party which prided itself on the efficiency of its extra parliamentary machine.[46]

Several points are worth making about these criticisms of Mr Heath. First, the criticisms were not acquiesced in by Diehards alone. Mr Heath's general mien clearly upset a lot of Conservatives irrespective of their policy views, and his leadership style went beyond the wide boundaries that Conservative ideas about authoritative leadership marked out. Second, the fact that Mr Powell was not a Conservative member of Parliament at the time of the leadership contest should not prevent us from grasping that much of the criticism levelled at Mr Heath in 1975 was merely a repetition of what Mr Powell had been saying (Europe and immigration aside) since 1972. In this sense, Mr William Whitelaw's prediction in 1969 that some other political figure might profit by Mr Powell's manoeuvres and climb on his shoulders proved remarkably accurate.[47] To exclude Mr Powell from the story of the 1975 leadership contest is like trying to erase Merlin from The Sword in the Stone or perhaps more appositely Delilah from the undoing of Samson. Third, however pertinent the Diehard cry that Mr Heath had deserted Conservative principles may have been, the charge was not a novel one, for it had been ritually invoked against numerous Conservative leaders. The most famous example was the assault on Peel's Conservatism by Disraeli. Disraeli complained that Peel always yielded to public opinion and never attempted to lead or form it. The alleged subsequent outcome was appeasement and the destruction of institutions clothed in the euphemism of 'the best bargain'.[48] This example takes on special interest when we observe the transplant of Disraelian phrases and ideas into the speeches and writing of Mr Powell. This was sometimes literal, as with the Turkish Admiral steering his fleet into the enemy harbour, and the 'tergiversation' of politicians; or conceptual, in the case of the importance of imagination, party, Parliament and the English character.[49] When at the top of the greasy pole himself, Disraeli became the object rather than the instigator of charges of ratting on Conservative principles. Writing anonymously in The Quarterly Review for 1860, for example, the future Lord Salisbury complained that Disraeli had never procured the triumphant assertion of Conservative principles or shielded ancient institutions from ruin. Instead, he had dragged his party into the ditch, by the use of strong discipline. Nine years later Salisbury was still writing of Disraeli's perpetual political mendicancy.[50] Clearly a reading of Conservative history demonstrates that if Mr Heath had deserted true Conservative principles then he had the consolation of being in good company. These good companions were not only deceased giants from a turbulent Conservative past. The charge of deserting Conservative principles was also raised against Conservative party leaders in the 1950s.[51] Amongst those most vocal in their criticism was yet another Lord Salisbury. Furthermore, if Mr Powell was correct and Mr Heath's determination to see the United Kingdom as a party to the Treaty of Rome did constitute a deviation from true Conservatism, then almost a generation of Conservatives, including Mr Harold Macmillan and R.A. (later Lord) Butler, shared in the 'guilt'.

Candidates and campaigns

The leadership campaign took its character from these criticisms of Mr Heath. The problem for the opponents of Mr Heath was not arguments to display against him, but finding an appropriate challenger to lay down the gauntlet. The Conservative party suffered from a dearth of likely leaders. In part this was due to Mr Heath's tendency to choose affable, like minded and somewhat colourless men as colleagues, but there was also an element of chance in the situation. By 1974, for example, many who had looked leadership material in 1970 were no longer eligible. Iain Macleod was dead, Mr Maudling had suffered eclipse through the proximity of the Poulson affair, and Mr Powell had ceased to be a Conservative MP. Of those who developed leadership potential after 1970, Mr Carr was discredited in Diehard quarters by his recent performance as shadow treasury spokesman, and had in any case indicated to colleagues his unwillingness to stand.[52] Another who had come into prominence after 1970 was Mr Whitelaw, but he was known to be extremely loyal to Mr Heath. In a statement from Central Office after the October election, Mr Whitelaw noted how his admiration and support for Mr Heath was well known and did not waver in difficult times. Such personal allegiance probably counted against Mr Whitelaw when he stood in the second ballot, as did his reputation for 'woolliness', which Lord Lambton suggested was fostered by supporters of Mr Heath.[53] The lack of serious contestants called forth several actual or aspiring candidates who were characterised either by their small claims on the leadership, or by their close association with Mr Heath. Amongst the former group were Mr Hugh Fraser and Mr Richard Wood. Mr Fraser was a Diehard who accurately described his challenge as modest, while Mr Wood was virtually unknown outside Westminster and his Bridlington constituency. Mr Wood conceded that some of his friends had ideas above his station in even talking about his nomination. There was also Sir Christopher Soames, Mr Julian Amery, Mr John Peyton and Sir Geoffrey Howe. Lord Alport thought little of Mr Amery's claim, and Sir Christopher Soames was both outside Parliament and personally unknown to most MPs. Both Mr Peyton and Sir Geoffrey Howe were candidates in the second ballot. In the latter group were Mr Whitelaw and Mr James Prior, both of whom contested Mrs Thatcher in the second ballot. Mr Prior suffered from his identification with Mr Heath, despite distancing himself after October 1974.[54]

This situation made Sir Keith Joseph the obvious if not the ideal candidate for the Diehards and those who thought the party had deviated from true Conservatism. Sir Keith was the obvious candidate because in the course of several thought provoking and well publicised speeches at Upminster, Leith, Preston and Leeds after the February election, he had adopted the Diehard cause, discovered that the past thirty years had been a decline into semi-socialism, and said that he accepted his share of responsibility for the errors and mistakes. He was not an ideal candidate for two reasons. The first was his peculiarly hesitant and self effacing manner, which for a short time was elevated to a desirable requisite of political leadership by his supporters. More important however, was the fact that, bound by constitutional convention, Sir Keith had been collectively responsible as a cabinet minister in the Heath administration for the very policies he was now proclaiming to be a deviation from Conservatism, and had chosen not to resign. In this sense, there was a certain irony, perhaps more, in Sir Keith (and later Mrs Thatcher) riding on the bandwagon of those who wanted to return to 'true' Conservatism.

The leadership bid by Sir Keith Joseph had the important effect of preventing Ditchers from trying quietly to replace Mr Heath by Mr Whitelaw without a contest immediately after the general election defeat in October 1974.[55] In other respects the Joseph candidature was less successful, and quickly came to grief. In Birmingham, on 19 October, while addressing himself to the limited possibility of successful state intervention, Sir Keith included a carelessly phrased sentence which claimed that 'The balance of our population, our human stock is threatened'. Ironically, this was succeeded textually by a call for caution in any moral crusade, because no one side had the whole of the argument. However, the opprobrium which surrounded the sentence itself increased doubts about the reliability of Sir Keith Joseph's judgement. As one Conservative whip commented, Sir Keith was a very brilliant man, but he had developed the habit of not always getting things quite right.[56] The speech effectively marked the end of Sir Keith Joseph's challenge, and he withdrew from the leadership race on the grounds of what he called personal unworthiness, and with the conviction that he had let the side down.[57]

The withdrawal of Sir Keith Joseph left either Mr Edward du Cann or Mrs Margaret Thatcher prepared to assume the Diehard mantle.

Mr du Cann was somewhat equivocal about his own candidature. Stories circulated that his reticence owed something to reports of past business activities which might be uncovered to damage both himself and the Conservative party.[58] Soundings in the City put the minds of some of his supporters at rest, but for a variety of personal and political reasons (including a feeling that he should not stand against Mrs Thatcher) Mr du Cann remained reluctant to stand. When he finally decided not to run (on 13 January 1975) about fifteen of his supporters including Mr Airey Neave and Sir Nigel Fisher went over to join Mrs Thatcher's camp. In order to maintain a united Diehard front, Mrs Thatcher had resisted efforts to make her step forward while Sir Keith Joseph was still in contention, but Sir Keith's withdrawal had removed that particular obstacle.[59]

Mrs Thatcher's campaign was organised by Mr Neave with Mr William Shelton as his principal lieutenant. The object of the Thatcher campaign was to capitalise on the grievances against Mr Heath. First, it was necessary to return to true Conservative principles, and Mrs Thatcher wrote expressing her conviction that the opportunity to project these principles had never been greater. Further, she explained that deviation from true Conservatism was one of the reasons for the party's electoral failure, since people believed that too many Conservatives had become socialists already.[60] In Mrs Thatcher's support, Sir Keith Joseph banged his Diehard drum, and wrote that in the course of his own lifetime, the Conservative party had strayed from its principles and instincts, and taken to semi-socialism. There was a need for the party to return to sound money, patriotism, thrift, the social market economy and middle class values. Mrs Thatcher emphasised that as these values — work, freedom, order — were supported across the social class spectrum, to sneer at them was to insult the working class no less than the bourgeoisie.[61] Second, emphasis was placed on the need for leaders to listen to their followers. In this way Mrs Thatcher demonstrated that she would not stray beyond the wide limits of authority to be entrusted to her. She explained to her constituents that this was where the Heath administration had gone wrong, since it had not listened enough to what supporters were saying.[62] In consequence the administration had allowed itself to become detached from many who had put their trust in it. Last, there was an attempt to display Mrs Thatcher as someone who would be able to create the aggressive spirit thought to be necessary to win a general election. In this attempt Mrs Thatcher was certainly assisted by her dazzling performances on the Finance Bill which was passing through Parliament in the course of the leadership election. It is ironical that Mr Heath's performances in the Finance Bill debates of 1965 worked in the same way for him.

The fight for the leadership was described by one member of

Mr Heath's Government as 'very bitter', with, as Lord Carrington conceded, a good deal of 'backbiting'.[63] Supporters of Mrs Thatcher placed much of the blame for this on the aggressive campaign managed on Mr Heath's behalf by Sir Timothy Kitson and Mr Kenneth Baker, with some help from Mr Peter Walker. They claimed that Mr Heath's supporters behaved with impropriety by being loud in their denigration of Sir Keith Joseph after his Birmingham speech, and by stirring up the allegation that Mrs Thatcher was a food hoarder following an interview she gave to the magazine *Pre-Retirement Choice*. It was also suggested that the Central Office machine was used in the partisan support of Mr Heath during the leadership campaign, and that the results of the National Union soundings, which proved to be heavily in favour of Mr Heath, were leaked to the press by the Heath camp.[64] Whether these events warranted the description 'dirty tricks' is open to question, and given the existing serious criticisms against Mr Heath, it is doubtful whether they were decisive. Nevertheless, such insensitivity won Mr Heath no new friends, and tended to reinforce doubts about his leadership style.

The main aim of Mr Heath's campaign was to try to juxtapose what his supporters saw as the national flavour of his post-1972 Ditcher policies, with what was seen to be the strictly middle class Diehard appeal of Mrs Thatcher. Time and again Mr Heath's supporters wheeled out Disraeli's aphorism that the Conservatives were a national party or nothing, to place in contrast with the Joseph-Thatcher fascination with market forces. The difficulty with this approach was that, under Mr Heath's leadership, in United Kingdom terms, the party had become less national in its electoral base than at any time since 1945. Mr Heath was also presented, and represented himself, as the man who had told the truth about the parlous economic state of the country in the October election. He would therefore be in a good position to lead the nation in the expected crisis to come. As Mr Whitelaw noted in the *CPC Monthly Report* for November 1974, the Conservatives could go forward in the knowledge that under Mr Heath's leadership, they had told the truth and not tried to hide facts about the economic crisis.

Given that two dozen Conservative MPs promised to support both Mrs Thatcher and Mr Heath in the first ballot on 4 February 1975,[65] a degree of uncertainty remains about exactly who supported whom. Mr Heath was probably supported in the first ballot by all the members of his shadow cabinet save Mrs Thatcher, Sir Keith Joseph and Mr Godber. However, as he had contravened acceptable ideas of authoritative leadership, violated what were seen to be true Conservative principles and failed to win political power, his chance of retaining the leadership was very slim. Doubters were alienated rather than converted by the bullying campaign run on his behalf. In these circumstances, Mrs Thatcher's victory in the first ballot by a margin insufficient to secure an outright win, was entirely unsurprising. Of course, the assumption here is that Conservative members of Parliament were neither stupid nor hypocritical, in the senses that, they did not vote in a random and haphazard manner, and that in their speeches, publications and quasi private intimations they expressed views which they could be said to have held. In other words it is assumed that the history of politics is something more than chance, and can be explained in terms of reasonable argument.[66] One problem of immense difficulty is to rank each of the criticisms of Mr Heath in order of importance. Is it possible, for example, to assert that Mr Heath's lack of electoral success meant that he would have lost the leadership election whatever his views about authority? It is possible but not profitable since the proposition is as hypothetical as 'What if Benjamin Disraeli had not been baptised?', or 'What if Sir Robert Peel had not been thrown from his horse and expired in agony in 1852?' All that can be asserted is that in the circumstances of electoral failure Mr Heath's deviation from traditional views about authoritative leadership and what he himself had defined as true Conservatism proved to be important rallying points for dissent.[67]

Having once secured a first ballot victory, Mrs Thatcher's conclusive triumph in the second ballot was made more likely by three intervening factors. The first was the general feeling that the contest had gone on long enough, and that further prolonged electioneering would do even more damage to party unity than had already been done. The second was that Mrs Thatcher was now viewed as the brave woman who had taken on Mr Heath, while everyone else (except Mr Fraser) had looked on. In part, this was unfair to some of the second ballot candidates who argued that their reason for not standing was that they wanted Mr Heath to win rather than because they were afraid of him. In any event, the fact that as many as four new candidates stepped forward did nothing to discourage the opinion that once the so called risky job of defeating Mr Heath had been achieved, the opportunists were now stepping in. Last, as previously explained, Mr Whitelaw and Mr Prior had been closely associated with Mr Heath, and a few days was too little time to establish an independent identity. The other contenders, Sir Geoffrey Howe and Mr Peyton were essentially lightweight candidates with no serious expectations of winning. On 11 February 1975 therefore, after the second ballot votes had been counted, Mrs Thatcher was announced the outright winner, 67 votes clear of her nearest rival, Mr Whitelaw. The Diehards had a new champion, the Conservative party had its sixth postwar leader, and for the first time the United Kingdom had a woman at the head of a major political party.

Notes

1   *The Spectator*, 9 March 1974.

2   Interview with Conservative MP, 26 February 1976.

3   Interview with Conservative MP, 21 October 1976.

4   Interview with Heath minister, 6 April 1977.

5   Raison, 'How the Tories can show their nerve', *The Daily Telegraph*, 6 October 1975.

6   Hailsham quoted in *The Daily Telegraph*, 20 March 1974.

7   Interview with Conservative MP, 8 June 1976.

8   Heath to Annual Dinner of 1922 Committee, quoted in *The Times*, 4 April 1974.

9   Cormack to Du Cann, quoted ibid., 9 May 1974.

10   Interview with Conservative MP, 8 June 1976.

11   Interview with shadow minister, 8 June 1976.

12   On the Figgures row and Adamson incident, see Hurd, *An End to Promises: Sketch of a Government 1970-74*, 1979, pp 133-4.

13   Butler and Kavanagh, *The British General Election of October 1974*, 1975, pp 62-6; Gilmour, 'The Tory dilemma that follows the election', *The Times*, 2 May 1974.

14   Carrington, 'Lessons for the future', *CPC Monthly Report*, April/May 1974; Cosgrave, 'The poisoned card', *The Spectator*, 4 May 1974; Gilmour, 'How Mr Heath could establish industrial harmony', *The Times*, 3 May 1974; Butler and Kavanagh, ibid., p.63.

15   Interview with Diehard shadow minister, 16 February 1978.

16   Interview with Heath shadow minister, 6 April 1977; Joseph, *Reversing the Trend*, 1975, p.63.

17   On Heath and the CPS see *The Daily Telegraph*, 5 July 1976.

18   Interview with shadow minister, 16 February 1978; interview with shadow minister, 6 April 1977.

19   Joseph, Preston, *The Times*, 6 September 1974.

20   Interview with shadow minister, 6 April 1977.

21   *Putting Britain First: a National Policy from the Conservatives*, 1974, pp 2, 12-13; ibid., pp 4, 6; ibid., pp 16-17.

22   King, *The Cecil King Diary, 1965-70*, 1972, pp 121, 145-6, 213, 240-1.

23   Butler and Kavanagh, op.cit., pp 43, 44, 66.

24   *Putting Britain First*, 1974, p.4.

25   Hayward to (Labour) candidates and election agents (private and confidential), 6 October 1974; Butler and Kavanagh, 1975, pp 44-50; ibid., pp 44, 124-6; Gale, 'The private anger of Edward Heath', *The New Statesman*, 11 October 1974.

26   Interview with Heath shadow minister, 8 June 1976; Heath,

Conservative Central Office *News Service*, (GE200) 6 October 1974.
27   Marten quoted in *The Daily Telegraph*, 16 October 1974; Hailsham quoted ibid., 18 October 1974.
28   Fisher, *The Tory Leaders: their Struggle for Power*, 1977, pp 147-9; ibid., p.151.
29   Interview with Heath shadow minister, 6 April 1977; Gardiner, *Margaret Thatcher from Childhood to Leadership*, 1975, p.168.
30   Rodgers quoted in Wood, 'Behind the leadership struggles', *The Times*, 20 January 1975; Home quoted in *The Daily Telegraph*, 3 February 1975.
31   Powell, 'Review of books', *The Spectator*, 13 October 1973.
32   Ibid.
33   Fisher, op.cit., p.158.
34   Disraeli, *Lord George Bentinck: a Political Biography*, 1852, pp 305, 306, 311, 316.
35   Interview with Conservative MP, 12 January 1978; interview with Conservative MP, 20 January 1978; Berkeley, *Crossing the Floor*, 1972, pp 108-9; interview with Conservative MP, 3 March 1971; Du Cann, quoted in 'London Diary', *The New Statesman*, 5 July 1974.
36   Biffen quoted in *The Sunday Times*, 10 November 1974.
37   Pinto-Duschinsky, 'Central Office and power in the Conservative party', *Political Studies*, 1972, p.7; Maxwell Fyfe report on party organisation, quoted in Wilson, 'Constituency party autonomy and central control', *Political Studies*, 1973, p.11.
38   Powell, 'Edward the Suppressor', *The Sun*, 3 February 1975; Fraser quoted in *The Sunday Telegraph*, 2 February 1975.
39   Cosgrave, 'Taking the machine apart', *The Spectator*, 20 April 1974; interview with member of Thatcher's private office, 17 November 1976.
40   Layton-Henry, 'Constituency authority in the Conservative party', *Parliamentary Affairs*, 1976, pp 398-400; Butler and Kavanagh, *The British General Election of February 1974*, 1974, p.208; Layton-Henry, op.cit., pp 396-7.
41   *A Better Tomorrow: the Conservative Programme for the Next Five Years*, 1970, Foreword by Heath, pp 2, 6.
42   *A Better Tomorrow*, 1970, pp 6, 13; Davies, *CCVR*, 1970, p.80; Heath, *CCVR*, 1970.
43   Biffen, 'Painful need to restate attitudes', *The Sunday Times*, 27 October 1974; Powell, 'Edward the Supressor', *The Sun*, 3 February 1975; Corfield, letters, *The Times*, 3 February 1975.
44   Powell, quoted in *The Times*, 30 November 1973; Fraser, quoted ibid., 21 January 1975; Powell, quoted in Ritchie (ed.), *Enoch Powell: a Nation or No Nation, Six Years in British Politics*, 1978, pp 39, 101.

45   Hailsham, quoted in *The Daily Telegraph*, 9 October 1974; Barber, *CCVR*, 1973; Powell, quoted in *The Times*, 30 November 1973; Powell, quoted ibid., 8 February 1974.
46   Marten, quoted in *The Daily Telegraph*, 16 October 1974 (see also Fisher, 1977, p.147); Quennell, letters, *The Times*, 3 April 1974.
47   Whitelaw, quoted in King, *The Cecil King Diary, 1965-70*, 1972, pp 241-2.
48   Disraeli, *Coningsby* (1844), 1967, pp 82, 292.
49   Ibid.; Powell, in Ritchie (ed.), *Enoch Powell: a Nation or No Nation*, 1978.
50   Salisbury, quoted in Monypenny and Buckle, *The Life of Benjamin Disraeli*, 1910-1920, vol.IV, pp 286-8, 11, 513.
51   Kilmuir, *Political Adventure: the Memoirs of the Earl of Kilmuir*, Weidenfeld and Nicolson, London 1964, pp 320-4; Johnson, *Cassandra at Westminster*, 1970, pp 54-63.
52   Interview with Heath minister, 6 April 1977.
53   Whitelaw, quoted in *The Daily Telegraph*, 18 October 1974; Lambton, 'Why Mr Heath should accept Sir Alec's terms for the election of a Tory leader', *The Times*, 20 January 1975.
54   Fraser, quoted in *The Times*, 21 January, 1975; Wood, quoted in Fisher, *The Tory Leaders*, 1977, p.160; Marten on Soames, quoted in *The Daily Telegraph*, 16 October 1974; Alport, letters, *The Times*, 28 January 1975.
55   Cosgrave, *Margaret Thatcher: a Tory and Her Party*, 1978, pp 36-7.
56   Interview with Conservative whip, 26 February 1976.
57   Cosgrave, 'Six months in the leadership', *The Spectator*, 6 September 1975.
58   Cosgrave, *Margaret Thatcher: a Tory and Her Party*, 1978, p.33; Fisher, *The Tory Leaders*, 1977, pp 160-3.
59   Fisher, ibid., p.163; interview with member of Thatcher's private office, 17 November 1976.
60   Thatcher, letter to constituents, quoted in *The Sunday Telegraph*, 2 February 1975; Thatcher, 'My Kind of Tory Party', *The Daily Telegraph*, 30 January 1975.
61   Joseph, 'My Kind of Tory Party', *The Daily Telegraph*, 28 January 1975; Thatcher, 'My Kind of Tory Party', ibid., 30 January 1975.
62   Thatcher, letter to constituents, quoted in *The Sunday Times*, 2 February 1975.
63   Interview with Heath minister, 8 June 1976; Carrington, quoted in *The Times*, 27 January 1975.
64   Gardiner, *Margaret Thatcher: from Childhood to Leadership*, 1975, p.166; Cosgrave, *Margaret Thatcher: a Tory and Her Party*, 1978, pp 51-3; Fisher, *The Tory Leaders*, 1978, p.171.

65   Interview with Conservative whip, 26 February 1976.
66   Elton, op.cit., p.126.
67   Interview with Conservative whip, 26 February 1976; interview with Conservative MP, 23 April 1979.

4 The Conservative party under Mrs Thatcher: the flight of the Iron Butterfly

'. . . his appointment by a Diehard leader appeared to be something of a declaration of intent. Nevertheless, if a week was a long time in politics, the seventeen years which had elapsed since this resignation were a good deal longer: and there is a sense in which Lord Thorneycroft had to spend his entire period as party chairman convincing a somewhat sceptical public that although in the Elysian Fields, he was certainly not dead'.

This chapter discusses the Conservative party under Mrs Thatcher's direction, and contrasts it with the party under the leadership of Mr Heath. A comparison is necessary to assess what changes took place after the leadership contest, and to see the extent to which Mrs Thatcher lived up to Diehard aspirations. Four areas are scrutinised including the policy making process within the party, party management and leadership style, the relationship between the centre and the localities in Conservative politics, and the financial relationship between the Conservative party and business. It is argued that claims by Mrs Thatcher and some of her Diehard supporters that she changed everything after becoming Conservative leader were gross exaggeration.[1] Changes wrought by Mrs Thatcher were never so radical as to threaten those parts of the traditional form of conversation which Mr Heath had upheld. For example, the making of policy remained where Mr Heath had left it: in the hands of the leader and those whom the leader chose to consult. In addition, the relations between the centre and the localities continued to operate in a way which deflected the local parties from over concern with expressly 'political' issues. In other ways too the party under Mrs Thatcher looked little different from the party Mr Heath had led. Business, finance and industry continued to grasp the Conservative party in a financial embrace which helped to ensure fidelity to private property and enterprise. Furthermore, the shadow cabinet remained anonymous and the advertising men continued to exercise an influence. Within limits however, important changes did take place. These were made to reassert those aspects of the traditional form of Conservative conversation from which

46

Mr Heath had deviated. For instance, Mrs Thatcher's leadership was more accessible and responsive to party opinion, and it checked the tendency of the centre to encroach on the activities of local associations. There were other changes as well. Mrs Thatcher was more circumspect in making policy commitments, generally more subtle in party management and more willing to seek to win hearts than Mr Heath had been. Last, morale in the parliamentary party and in the local associations improved considerably.

The evolution of policy

An observer unfamiliar with the unspoken rules of Conservative politics might be forgiven for thinking that when Mrs Thatcher wrote to her constituents on the eve of the leadership election asserting that Conservatives had not listened enough to their own supporters in the Heath years (see above, p.39) she was envisaging some greater role for the annual conference of the National Union. It had, after all, been condemned in 1969 as a stage managed farce. It is true that Mrs Thatcher was extremely careful to be seen at many conference sessions after 1975, but the careful management of Conservative conferences continued as if the leadership election had never actually taken place.

Two of the best examples of conference management after 1975 concerned the debate on economic policy in Brighton in 1978, and the industrial relations debate in Blackpool the previous year. At Brighton a deliberately vague motion concerning economic policy and taxation was chosen. At a time when incomes policy was at the focus of attention following the Government's call for a 5 per cent limit on wages, the motion evaded the issue entirely, and called for a reduction in the burden of direct taxation. A call to reduce direct taxation at a Conservative annual conference has all the uncertainty of a Methodist convention debating sin, and the genuine divisions in the party over the appropriateness of incomes policy were left to dribble out in the radio and television studios.[2] At Blackpool in 1977 Mr James Prior won the backing of representatives for a speech in which he defended the official position that the Conservatives were opposed to the closed shop, even though they did not think that the time was right to outlaw it. Conference management manifested itself in several ways. First, the motion discussed was 'woolly and pretty pale beige'. It called for a change in the law on the closed shop to protect the right of workers employed before union membership agreements were made, and to give more consideration to those people who did not want to join a union.[3] As the motion called for a change in the law Mr Prior might easily have chosen to oppose it, but he assumed (in a somewhat cavalier

47

fashion) that the motion was in keeping with official policy. Considering that Mr Prior spoke in favour of the motion and considering that the motion called for a change in the law, both those in favour and against outlawing the closed shop could reasonably support it. Second, despite the fact that amendments were submitted specifically calling for the banning of the closed shop, not one was called. Third, one Conservative MP claimed that the conference chairman was inundated with slips from Conservative trade unionists requesting to speak in support of Mr Prior.[4] No sinister motive was attached to this by a CTU national official who maintained that it was not possible to rig the debate. However, he did concede that 'sections in the party, especially the CTU, had planned to give Mr Prior a good reception' adding that as things turned out this wasn't necessary.[5] Without denying that Mr Prior won the day through sheer argument, it is apparent that the cards were heavily stacked in his favour and that the leadership was reluctant to rely on argument alone.

Following the 1977 conference, Mr Fred Silvester MP complained that the conference organisers were still playing their old tune, and treating the party like a 'nanny' treats an infant. Mr Silvester did not want the conference to decide policy, but as it was supposed to advise, he thought that representatives had to have an opportunity to express that advice. Instead, the party was 'so concerned to avoid embarrassing defeats and splits that the organisers shepherd the party around'. One Conservative MP considered that this shepherding was in fact more pronounced than it had been in the Heath years. In the late 1960s if anyone had tried to stampede the platform as the CTU had done at Blackpool, they would have been given short shrift.[6] For members of Mrs Thatcher's shadow cabinet however, the concern expressed at the increased tendency to manage National Union conferences was not really a problem. They saw little role for the conference in party policy making, and thought conference management necessary because it allowed the best available use of television time. Even those who ascribed to themselves the term populist in the shadow cabinet regarded the conference as nothing other than a 'demonstration exercise'. This was because representatives were not a good cross sample of the people likely to vote Conservative. Therefore while conference had the superficial appearance of being democratic, and while it might occasionally be given its head, it was not a suitable vehicle for the formation of policy.[7]

Mrs Thatcher's shadow ministers emphasised the decisive role that the leadership played in the evolution of policy. They dressed this mode of conduct up as an imperative by doffing their bowlers to Burke and stressing the hurly-burly of the political world. The essential task of the opposition was to carry out a 'crusading' role and this meant (they believed that) shadow ministers were so busy travelling round the country making speeches and responding to events, that it was very difficult to consult satisfactorily or to have a co-ordinated strategy. As one shadow minister observed 'we live from day to day'.[8] Conservative policy seems to have been determined by the leadership within the context of the broad disposition of Conservative feelings, and modified by recourse to opinion polls, by-election results and talking to people. One shadow minister thought that the mistake of the media and the academics was to imagine that policy evolved from a background of long and studied reflection, whereas often nothing of the kind occurred. To be sure the 1976 policy document *The Right Approach* was drawn together by Mr Angus Maude and Mr Christopher Patten in the Conservative research department on the basis of work done by policy groups. However, the 1977 document *The Right Approach to the Economy* was simply the work of five members of the shadow cabinet who, according to one of their colleagues, just went away and wrote it. This was not very different from what had happened under Mr Heath towards the end of his leadership. For example, the Conservative pledge in 1974 to set up an indirectly elected Scottish assembly rather than a directly elected one, was the product not of careful strategy but of the endeavours of 'poor Gordon Campbell, who had three hours in a dimly lit room to draw up a policy'.[9]

The role of the leader in policy formation was crucial, and as party leader Mrs Thatcher appeared no less willing than Mr Heath to fly policy kites. In September 1977, for example, in a television interview, Mrs Thatcher suggested that faced with a circumstance similar to the 1974 miners' strike, in the last resort the Conservatives might hold a referendum. This was an initiative taken without the knowledge of her shadow cabinet. It had come 'out of the blue', probably from briefings with members of the Thatcher private office.[10] This wide leadership discretion allowed a peripheral role for the policy groups operating from Parliament and serviced by the Conservative research department. The groups were set up by shadow ministers who developed policy in their own functional areas, and by Sir Keith Joseph who was in overall charge of the process. The number of committees ranged from about 50 in early 1976 to more than 80 in 1977. The bulk of their work was done by the beginning of 1978. The groups took on the same role as they had done before 1970 though they tended to be smaller — one of the energy groups was attended by a group of between ten and twelve — and in general there were fewer non-members of Parliament on them.[11] Complaints were made after 1975, just as they had been made before then, that policy evolution took place with too little consultation. Although after Mrs Thatcher's elevation a careful attempt was made to include any

MP who wanted to play a part in the process, criticism surfaced that the party was 'virtually paralysed' as a policy making body, and that it had gone in for 'isolated thinking'.[12] The activities of Sir Keith Joseph were said to be 'shrouded in mystery', and some MPs regarded him as a recluse. Conservative members expressed the view that they were making little contribution to party policy and that they therefore had no alternative but to plough their own furrows. These criticisms have a familiar ring when compared with the assaults on Mr Heath for lack of consultation and failure to win acquiescence.[13]

Central-local relations

The nature of central-local relations under Mrs Thatcher stayed essentially as it had been under Mr Heath. The elitist nature of the conversation in Conservative politics continued to be reinforced by the minimal political role allowed to local party associations, and their supreme task of raising revenue for the party at the centre remained unaltered. Vigorous attempts to break out of this pattern had been made in the late 1960s, when the Greater London Young Conservatives launched a campaign to radically politicise the National Union. They proposed that a political committee should be set up in every local association to give an institutional focus to the discussion of politics in the locality. This would have replaced and enlarged upon the role of the functional and client groups which operated on the periphery of local associations and which were concerned, for example, with trade unions and local government. They also called for greater control to be exercised by local associations in the selection and re-selection of Conservative candidates. In response to this initiative, the National Union executive committee set up a review committee under Lord Chelmer to investigate if the Conservative party outside Parliament might be made more democratic. Such was the interest in the issue that only five Conservative members of Parliament and fourteen constituency associations submitted evidence. Lord Chelmer produced certain watered down proposals but even these were quietly removed at a central council meeting in October 1973, through the energetic activity of Mr Edward du Cann and two senior figures within the National Union, Sir John Taylor and Lord Clyde Hewlett.[14] While Mr du Cann was an Alpini on the battlefield of Parliament's fight to control the executive,[15] he and his colleagues in the 1922 Committee were evidently more circumspect about the idea of local political committees debating policy and controlling Conservative candidates and members of Parliament. Such a large measure of politicisation might deflect local parties from their duties of filling the party coffers and

50

bringing out the voters on election day.

Although the Conservative party rejected the idea that discussion of political issues should become the dominant activity of the local associations, a degree of politicisation did take place. It was stimulated by the Hon. Sara Morrison who was party vice-chairman between 1971 and 1975. Sara Morrison was well aware that the days when local associations needed to do nothing more than raise revenue and drum up support on election day were gone. There was a need to 'take positive steps to sow the seeds of understanding and party allegiance between elections' within the community. The way to do this was to articulate an 'intelligible political ethos' in reaching out to youth and special interest groups. Institutional devices deployed to meet this aim included a central employment scheme for agents to enable the party to make the best use of scarce resources, and the reorganisation of the youth department at Central Office.[16]

There was hardly any disagreement with these broad aims in Mrs Thatcher's Central Office. Politicisation continued within the constraint that the primary task of local associations was organisation for elections and fund raising. The phrase 'to sow the seeds of understanding' within the community was ritually invoked on many occasions after 1975, and the importance of developing a dialogue with youth and special interest groups was particularly emphasised. The key institutional vehicle for this development was the emergence of the Department of Community Affairs under the direction of Mr Andrew Rowe. Mr Rowe had originally been appointed in January 1975 to improve the contact between the Conservative party and voluntary service groups. Various responsibilities subsequently accrued to him including the task of improving relations with minority groups, the encouragement of the youth side of the party, the development of an organisation for Conservative trade unionists and the operation of a small business bureau. In the view of a senior official responsible for community affairs, the role of the department was to make the party more aware of and confident in handling discernible and definable groups, and 'to let the party know that brown and black men are here to stay'. This was important from an electoral point of view because 'we can't win if we remain ignorant of the way trade unions, coloured men and young people work'.[17]

The impact of the Department of Community Affairs was hampered by financial restrictions which meant that Mr Rowe had to operate with a skeleton staff of less than two dozen. Nevertheless various client and functional groups emerged or were strengthened. To improve relations with minority groups, for example, an Anglo-Asian Conservative Society and an Anglo-West Indian Society were set up in 1976.[18] In addition the activities of the Federation of Conservative Students were expanded, and the 70 branches which existed in 1974 were increased to nearly 200 in 1978, with a membership of 16,000.[19] The most dramatic development was the resurrection of the Conservative Trade Unionists' Department. In the postwar period Conservative activity in the trade unions on an organised basis had been minimal. Advisory committees of volunteers existed up and down the country and at various times there were between 15 and 50 part-time organisers operating. Each year a conference for Conservative trade unionists was held, but in 1974 the small CTU Department in Central Office fell victim to economy measures, and the two national organisers were retired. The CTU Department at Central Office was re-established in 1975 at the instigation of Lord Thorneycroft, the party chairman appointed by Mrs Thatcher. Lord Thorneycroft considered that it was vital to keep in touch with trade union feeling and so two full-time national organisers were appointed, and five field agents, four full-time and one part-time. The aims of the CTU were said to be to improve communication between the Conservative party and the unions, to increase understanding about trade unions within the Conservative party, and to eradicate the political character of the trade union movement itself.[20] How far these objects were achieved is discussed in chapter 5, but by 1978 the CTU had 280 groups, and was attracting considerable interest.

In general how significant was the growth of the Community Affairs Department? In the first place, the blossoming of a variety of functional and client groups at the centre with counterparts in the local parties safeguarded the primacy of what Conservatives saw as the essentially organisational nature of constituency associations. As long as these groups were diverse and on the periphery of local associations rather than amalgamated into a single political committee, they constituted no threat to the traditional form of Conservative conversation. Second, some Diehards believed that Mr Rowe was a sinister knight, clothed in the armour of progressivism and he encountered a lot of hostility as he built up the department. Others were unclear what the department was actually doing in part because although Mr Rowe had addressed the 1922 Committee there was not a great deal of contact between his staff and the parliamentary party. Clearly, however, Mr Rowe had powerful allies for his activities in the personages of Mrs Thatcher and Lord Thorneycroft, the party chairman. One senior official felt that this support had enabled the department to convince constituency parties of the need to be more tolerant of immigrants, and Conservative trade unionists were convinced that due to the intervention of Lord Thorneycroft, they had more of a place in the sun than ever before.[21]

The reverse of the political ethos coin concerned finance. Finance was the dominant theme in the relations between the centre and the local parties, and the severe financial difficulties of the party at the centre after 1974 served to underline the importance of the revenue raising role of the local associations. The constituencies continued to send in contributions with the same endeavour that they had done under Mr Heath. The seriousness of the financial situation made Mrs Thatcher's choice of party chairman more than usually important. The nomination of Lord Thorneycroft caused a good deal of surprise. As Peter Thorneycroft MP, Lord Thorneycroft's most celebrated action had been to resign from the treasury in 1958 in protest against what he saw as the inflationary tendencies of Conservative policies. In this respect his appointment by a Diehard leader appeared to be something of a declaration of intent. Nevertheless, if a week was a long time in politics, the seventeen years which had elapsed since this resignation were a good deal longer; and there is a sense in which Lord Thorneycroft had to spend his entire period as party chairman convincing a somewhat sceptical public that although in the Elysian Fields, he was certainly not dead. (When asked how he enjoyed his elevation from the House of Commons to the House of Lords, the Earl of Beaconsfield replied, 'I am dead: dead but in the Elysian Fields'.)

The Conservative financial crisis had been precipitated by a combination of excessive spending and reduced income. Expenditure by the party at the centre in the financial year 1973 (which ended 31 March 1974) exceeded £2 million and surpassed spending for any year since the party began publishing its accounts in 1967. The party treasurers explained this in terms of a more than usually prolonged build-up to the February 1974 general election. In 1974 expenditure rose again by more than £700,000. This time the increase was put down to the indecisive February result which caused expenditure to be sustained at election level for many months in anticipation of the October election. This had not happened in the wake of the 1970 election. While expenditure increased, revenue fell away. Although the total central income for 1973 approached £3 million, and was more than enough to meet spending, Conservative supporters were not as responsive to the October 1974 election appeal as they had been to the February appeal. Furthermore, following the October election donations slumped as is normal in the year following an election appeal. In consequence expenditure exceeded income by more than £1¼ million in the financial year 1974, and in the first five months of 1975 the party ran up a deficit of £75,000 each month. This reduced cash and reserves to the perilously small total of £270,000 by the end of August 1975.[22]

Two strategies were launched to wipe out this deficit. The first involved retrenchment. Taking 1974 as the base financial year, expenditure was sliced by one-third in 1975, one-quarter in 1976, and in 1977 — inflation notwithstanding — it was held level. What Lord

Thorneycroft called 'some pretty drastic economies' were made, notably at Central Office. In 1975, for example, about £300,000 was cut from the Central Office staff and activities budget. This included the laying off of staff, the removal of the telex machine and the slashing of expense accounts to beer and sandwiches level.[23] Central publicity was particularly hit (see p. 57) and in general the effect on morale at Central Office was deleterious.

The second strategy involved increasing revenue, and Lord Thorneycroft urged the local associations to concentrate their efforts in this direction. Between 1969 and 1974, under Mr Heath, constituency contributions constituted variously between one-tenth and one-third of total central income. In the first three years under Mrs Thatcher they constituted between one-quarter and one-third of central income. (From the financial year 1975, the Conservative party received an annual state grant of about £150,000 towards parliamentary services inside the Palace of Westminster. To effect comparison with the Heath years this amount has been deducted from total central income in calculating the fractional proportion of constituency contributions.) In the first full year of the Thatcher leadership, 1975, constituency contributions doubled on the previous year to £570,000. This helped to boost revenue to just under £2 million which, while sufficient to meet expenditure, was too little to expand activities and increase the pay of professional staff.[24] In pursuit of extra subscriptions (and more members) Lord Thorneycroft launched a national campaign called 'Link up with the Conservatives', which ran from September to November 1976. Egged on by Central Office, the good ladies of the Conservative associations embarked upon a heady round of sponsored knitting, tart and tipple lunches, county balls, ox roasting and champagne suppers in the Conservative cause. This produced some rather expanded waistlines, diverted the localities from more controversial 'political' activity like calling members of Parliament to account, and boosted the total of constituency contributions for 1976 to £587,000. In all the years before, only the Carrington appeal in the salad days of Mr Heath's leadership had produced more. Contributions rose again in 1977, and following an £80,000 deficit the previous year, the party went back into surplus.[25]

The nature of central-local relations in Conservative politics was not then fundamentally altered when Mrs Thatcher replaced Mr Heath: local parties were encouraged to articulate a political ethos but reminded that their overriding task was to raise revenue.

Business, industry, finance and the Conservative party

Apart from constituency donations, a large proportion of the central income of the Conservative party derived from direct subscribers who were either individuals or companies. The pattern of donations made by business, industry and finance to Conservative party funds continued under Mrs Thatcher in much the same way as it had developed in the last years of Mr Heath's leadership. The extent of business contributions to the Conservative party has been a source of perennial argument in party politics. The Conservative party has maintained that, contrary to popular belief, it has not been heavily dependent on big business. It has not seen fit however, to disclose a list of corporate donors to central funds, nor to distinguish between corporate and individual donations in its published annual accounts. Even if this had been done, there are problems which make analysis imprecise. First, the financial years of some corporate donors and of the Conservative party do not coincide. It is not always possible therefore to know the precise year that donations from these companies were included in the Conservative accounts. Second, section 19 of the 1967 Companies Act requires corporations to disclose contributions in excess of £50 to political parties and 'persons carrying on activities which can reasonably be regarded as likely to affect support for a political party'. These provisions do not however cover industrialist councils, which attract funds from business and industry, and quietly dispose of several hundred thousand pounds each year. It is therefore hard to assess how much money found its way into Conservative party coffers through, for instance, the 'laundered' route of one of the industrialist councils, the British United Industrialists. This was formed in 1966 to support anti-socialist activities. Third, the published party accounts reported only that revenue raised by the Conservative party at the centre. Party officials have estimated that constituency contributions to the centre amount to only about one-eighth of the income raised by local associations to meet their own requirements. Without inspecting a large number of local constituency accounts an assessment cannot be made of the extent to which this local income is generated by contributions from local enterprises not bound to disclose political donations. A proportion of this local income is sent to central funds, and although it appears in the accounts as constituency contributions, that does not necessarily mean that part of it has not been derived from business or industrial sources.[26]

Such uncertainties notwithstanding, certain observations of a limited value can be made about business contributions to the Conservative party with Mrs Thatcher as leader. Taking the first three years of her leadership, traceable business contributions constituted about one-third of central income (state grant excluded). In 1975, contributions fell by £300,000 on the previous year to under £600,000. This seems to have owed less to the change in leadership and more to three special circumstances. In the first place two general elections in 1974 had prompted companies to be more than usually responsive to entreaties from the party treasurers. It was likely therefore that the succeeding year would prove less remunerative for the party. In addition, in 1975 there was a competing attraction for funds in the form of the EEC referendum campaigns. Large firms made special contributions nearing £1 million to 'Britain in Europe', which diminished the amount available for other political causes.[27] Third, some attempt was made by the Liberal party in the wake of their general election successes in 1974 to seduce industrialists away from contributing to Conservative party funds. In March 1975 Mr Thorpe, the Liberal leader, gave an evening reception in his Bayswater home to about two dozen chieftains of industry and finance. While no homberg was passed around Mr Thorpe discussed the prospects of electoral reform, and subsequently reminded them that the Conservative party had become 'paralytic' about the business contributions it received. The effect of this appeal is difficult to gauge but one of those in attendance, Sir Kenneth Keith, who was linked both to Rolls Royce and Hill Samuel pointed out that a number of industrialists like himself had lost confidence in the Conservative party, and that the party had a lot of thinking to do.[28]

Despite these special circumstances, the pattern of contributions in 1975 turned out to be not very different from 1976 or 1977. Indeed in each of these three years large contributions were received from the same specific areas of the economy. While Mr Harold Macmillan complained in 1936 that the Conservative party was dominated in part by second class brewers, there was no indication in the 1970s that the brewers led the way in financial donations. The biggest contributions tended to come from engineering, chemical, building and food manufacturing concerns. There was also strong support from city institutions, including insurance, banking and finance houses. In each of the three years beginning with 1975, the engineering industry contributed about £90,000, the chemical industry about £57,000, food manufacturers something close to £50,000, and the building industry approximately £40,000. In the same period banking and finance houses averaged £80,000 each year, and insurance companies about £70,000. How does this compare with the Heath era? In the last two years of the Heath leadership almost exactly the same sectors of enterprise were the principal fairy godmothers to Conservative Central Office.[29] The reliability of contributions from specific areas owed a good deal to the loyalty which certain large business and industrial concerns showed to the Conservative party. After 1974 the major donors were Guest, Keen and Nettlefold, the engineering company, which gave a total of £70,000, the Rank Organisation (£60,000) Tate and Lyle (£50,000) British and Commonwealth Shipping (£45,000) and Ranks Hovis Macdougall (£45,000). Other large donors included the builders, Newarthill (£27,000) and the bankers Baring Brothers (£25,000). Each of these firms had donated substantial sums in the last two years of the Heath leadership. (In 1973 and 1974 GKN donated a total of £68,000, the Rank Organisation gave £75,000, the Beecham Group gave £20,000, Tate and Lyle contributed £36,000 and British and Commonwealth Shipping donated £32,000. Of the other firms, Ranks Hovis Macdougall contributed £25,000, Newarthill gave £44,000 and Baring Brothers donated £25,000.)[30] It seems clear that a change in personnel at the top of the Conservative party had a negligible effect on business contributions. The embrace between the political and economic manifestations of private enterprise continued uninterrupted.

In other respects, the Conservative party changed very little with the election of Mrs Thatcher. Mr Heath's leadership had been criticised by Diehards for the influence that it gave to the gentlemen of the advertising profession. Under Mrs Thatcher the influence of the advertising men continued, despite some early indications that affairs would be different. Indeed, after 1978 an advertising agency was given wider control over Conservative publicity than at any time since Colman, Prentis and Varley influenced propaganda in the 1959 general election. The advertising men had a quiet introduction. As the newly elected leader in 1975, Mrs Thatcher was concerned to lose some of the abrasiveness associated with her since she had been protrayed as a penny-pinching milk-snatcher in 1971. To this end, Mr Gordon Reece, who had been advising the Conservative party on broadcasting since 1967 was appointed to Mrs Thatcher's private office. Mr Reece's job — he was on secondment from EMI — was to advise Mrs Thatcher how to present herself more naturally. Slowly but perceptively the ministrations worked. Mrs Thatcher's vocal delivery became more relaxed and her hairstyle took on a softer form. With a little help from Lady Tilney Mrs Thatcher's dress sense was assisted too. By a combination of practice and a change in cosmetics the Iron Butterfly lost some of her metallic exterior.[31]

From this small beginning Mr Reece's influence blossomed. In February 1978 he replaced Mr Tom Hooson as director of communications at Conservative Central Office. Following the financial crisis at Central Office the Conservative party had drastically cut the amount of money spent on publicity. While nearly £1 million was spent in the financial year 1974, this was pruned to £150,000 in 1975, £200,000 in 1976, and £275,000 in 1977. This retrenchment handicapped Mr Hooson's scope and by the beginning of 1978 Conservative

MPs were becoming worried by the insignificance of the publicity effort.[32] Following the appointment of Mr Reece, the three advisory committees of sympathetic publicity experts and politicians that operated under Mr Hooson were scrapped and the advertising agency Saatchi and Saatchi Garland-Compton were appointed to handle all advertising and publicity. Saatchi and Saatchi set about marketing the Conservative party in a vigorous way. In place of the run-of-the-mill television broadcasts devoted to politicians being honest and reasonable, professional actors were employed to give novelty and impact to the Conservative message. In cinemas, young courting couples relishing the splendid isolation of the back row of the stalls, were suddenly exhorted from the screens to put their trust in Mrs Thatcher; and in towns and cities up and down the country over a thousand giant and prominent posters relayed to the masses the observation that 'Labour isn't working'. The hoardings were acquired in the summer of 1978 after grocery manufacturers and brewers — acting from a mixture of political and commercial motives — had liberated space at short notice. This particular campaign cost £67,000 and prompted an official but unsuccessful Labour party complaint to the Advertising Standards Authority.[33]

The Saatchi campaigns were successful at least in the sense that the marketing of parties became something of a political issue. They caused questions to be asked about the amount and type of advertising that was suitable. Mr Tony Benn, for instance, estimated with some unease that the Conservatives would be spending up to £2 million on advertising in the run-up to the general election, and Mr Dennis Healey declared that Mrs Thatcher had relegated the Conservative party to a property 'to be sold like soap powder'. In addition, Mr Merlyn Rees, the Home Secretary, complained that Conservative advertisements on law and order had been compiled by advertising agents 'and not by people who really understand crime'.[34]

The Conservative response was a mixture of glee that so many Labour feathers had been ruffled and studied incomprehension that anyone should consider the marketing of parties unusual. While Mr Angus Maude expressed the former sentiment precisely when he told a party meeting in Warwickshire that nothing had lately given the party so much pleasure as the Labour attack, Mr Norman Fowler (shadow transport spokesman) and Lord Thorneycroft vied with each other in their efforts to see what all the fuss was about. Mr Fowler pointed out that press and information officers in Whitehall cost £8 million each year, and Lord Thorneycroft remarked that there was nothing extraordinary in deploying professional experts to project the Conservative party image.[35]

What appears salient is that despite the innocent rejoinders and

58

despite previous Diehard criticism of Mr Heath, in the cou
Thatcher leadership the role of professional experts in mark
gradually increased. In 1976, for example, a member of Mrs Thatcher's
private office pointed out that a major difference between the Thatcher
and Heath leaderships was that under Mrs Thatcher people like
Mr Gordon Reece — at that time an adviser concerned only with
Mrs Thatcher's personal image — knew that they were to have nothing
to say about policy.[36] Ironically, little more than twelve months later
Mr Reece had been placed in complete charge of Conservative publicity
and the dissemination of Conservative propaganda. It might be argued
that even this promotion left Mr Reece and Saatchi and Saatchi removed from actual policy making. This however assumes a clear line
can be drawn between the making and marketing of policy. As marketing involves a degree of interpretation of the product such a neat
disjunction seems unlikely. Mr William Whitelaw doubtless reflected on
this when, confronted on BBC television in the spring of 1979 with a
Conservative law and order advertisement, he indicated that he bore
responsibility only for policy and not for the implications arising from
advertisements. In the end Mr Reece came a long way from advising
about eye shadow. Under him the discretion a professional advertising
agency had over propagating the Conservative message was greater
than any agency had under Mr Heath. Given this, one might reasonably
conclude that by courtesy of Mrs Thatcher the advertising nexus had
never had it so good.

There was also some similarity between the performance of
Mrs Thatcher's shadow cabinet and that of her predecessor — both
started badly, then faded. After 1974 widespread dissatisfaction was
voiced in the parliamentary party and in the party in the country at
the inability of shadow ministers to make any kind of impact. From
inside the House of Commons, Mr Robert McCrindle complained that
there was unanimity in the view that the shadow cabinet, with few
exceptions, was unconvincing and second rate in comparison to the
likes of Mr Callaghan, Mr Foot, Mr Healey and Mrs Williams. The
Diehard Mr Nicholas Fairburn went somewhat further when he suggested that there were too many wallflowers on the front bench who
were united by their anonymity.[37] Outside Parliament criticism was
no less strong. The secretary of the Diehard Selsdon group spoke of the
'palsied lack of will of our own front bench', while Mr Jimmy Gordon
of the Ditcher Tory Reform Group lamented the lack of vigour, drive
and leadership in the shadow cabinet. From constituency parties came
motions critical of the 'shadowless cabinet' and the limited impact of
Her Majesty's opposition. These were submitted to party meetings, and
to conferences of the National Union, and the suggested ineffectiveness
of the opposition was even debated at the 1975 annual conference.[38]

...dow cabinet there was recognition that little
...e. Mr John Peyton, for instance, acknowledged
...d so far to catch and hold the attention of the
...e noted that previous shadow cabinets had been
...ed. Two shadow spokesmen and one Conservative MP
...the lack of impact, but stressed that while it was a little
...was not particularly important. They each pointed out that
...shadow cabinet had been equally anonymous. Not only had
th... ...vernment stolen the limelight before 1970, but certain Conservative backbenchers had been more successful at getting newspaper
coverage than their own front bench colleagues. The splash caused by
Mr Peter Walker after 1974 was no more than the waves created by
Mr Duncan Sandys before 1970. In general the feeling in the parliamentary party was strong that exposure in opposition was a difficult
commodity to grab hold of whoever happened to be the party leader.
One Conservative whip stressed that this was particularly true for the
Conservatives in opposition since they had long been bereft of com-
municators and laden with gentlemen skilled in the managerial arts.[39]

The flight of the Iron Butterfly

Mrs Thatcher did however preside over some important changes in the
Conservative party. To begin with the leadership became extremely
circumspect about making explicit commitments, in contrast to the
problem solving emphasis of the Heath years. This circumspection was
founded upon three suppositions about the nature of social change in
Britain. The first involved an appreciation that certain social problems
were much less soluble than others, and certainly more insoluble than
Conservatives in 1970 had thought them to be. For Sir Geoffrey Howe,
for example, this meant that there was more to be said than he had
once thought 'for a degree of patience, for a determination to arouse
fewer expectations that may not be swiftly fulfillable'.[40] Encouraged
by Mr Angus Maude at the Conservative research department, Conservatives appeared to appreciate more keenly that law was a limited
tool in the engineering of social change, and that blueprints containing
legal remedies suffered from rigidity in the face of diverse and complicated arrangements in society. Even when laws were established to
outlaw what were to Conservatives unacceptable practices like the
closed shop, there was no guarantee that they would have the desired
effect.[41] Second, Conservatives began to appreciate that as the world
was changing so rapidly, detailed plans worked out in opposition might
be irrelevant or unsuitable by the time the party came to power. One
Conservative MP, for instance, noted in 1976 that to produce detailed

proposals for dealing with the problems of 'an altogether different and even unpredictable tomorrow' would be folly and likely to end in disaster.[42] Both Mr Douglas Hurd and Sir Ian Gilmour agreed, and Mr Hurd pointed out such lack of circumspection by the Conservatives in 1970 had proved costly.[43] Third, hesitancy about policy commitments was reinforced by the view that the stream of legislation already passed by Parliament had undermined respect for the idea of law and led to the British people being exhausted by bold new initiatives and zigzag changes of policy.[44]

The hesitancy about policy commitment helps to explain the second substantial difference between Mrs Thatcher's leadership and Mr Heath's. While Prime Minister Mr Heath had consciously shied away from general reflection about the nature of Conservatism: with Mrs Thatcher the reverse was the case. By articulating what she understood to be the broad tenets of Conservative philosophy, she was seen to be responding to Diehard cries for a return to true Conservative principles, but it was also a device to steer the party clear of specific promises. In addition, concentration on the fundamental aspects of Conservative thought diverted attention from those policy issues on which the party was clearly divided. The general orientation of Mrs Thatcher's reflections was Diehard. In her party conference speeches Mrs Thatcher stressed that too much emphasis had been placed in the past on economic problems and not enough on moral and political questions which were at the root of economics. The Conservative party was not without blemish in this respect, with the result that while all too often they had won the arguments, they had failed to win the hearts and the votes of the electorate. In attending to this imbalance Mrs Thatcher concentrated on a moral defence of free enterprise, pointing out that it was the only system likely to preserve fundamental rights or freedoms. These included the right of people to work, within wide limits, at whatever they chose and wherever they wished, the right to own property, to have the state as servant, and the right of people to reflect their 'natural' inequality.[45] What was peculiarly Diehard about this appeal was the juxtaposition of the free society with the nastiness of socialism, and the explicit assertion that citizens could have one or the other, but that there was no middle ground. The contention that 'genuine' Conservatism rather than milk and water socialism was the best reply to 'full-bloodied' socialism showed the regularity with which Mrs Thatcher worshipped at the shrine of Hayek. The socialist menace came from a Labour party 'now committed to a programme which is frankly and unashamedly Marxist' and difficult to distinguish from Communism.[46] There were only two possible choices for people. They could either follow Labour along the road to a Britain modelled on Eastern Europe ('Britain beware. The

61

signpost reads "This way to the total Socialist state"') or they could respond to a Conservative party now determined to appeal to 'the deepest instincts of our people'. If they chose the latter, citizens would be joining with a party freshly embarked upon a crusade to stop the onward march of socialism once and for all, and a party which, through the injection of Diehard rectitude was once again a vehicle for the hopes and interests of working people.[47] By the projection of this message Mrs Thatcher was seen by one of her supporters in the shadow cabinet as a genuine populist articulating the views of ordinary people. A less effusive interpretation came from a Ditcher member of Parliament who observed that Mrs Thatcher was an ideologue, who believed in the forces of light confronting the forces of darkness, and who really did think that socialism was evil.[48]

Mrs Thatcher's Diehard leanings caused her to gather around the leader Conservatives of a similar political ilk. To help in the preparation of speeches Diehard writers like Dr Patrick Cosgrave, Mr Alfred Sherman and Mr T.E. Utley were called in. They were encouraged to obtain information from the Diehard Centre for Policy Studies rather than the Conservative research department. Mrs Thatcher also relied upon Diehard MPs like Mr Norman Tebbit and Mr George Gardiner for political intelligence. However, the Diehard influence should not be overstated. It is important to register that the third difference between the leadership of Mrs Thatcher and the leadership of Mr Heath was the attempt the former made to balance out the shadow cabinet between the different view points in the party.

One of Mrs Thatcher's earliest actions as leader was to dismiss six Ditchers from the shadow cabinet. These were Mr Peter Walker, Mr Robert Carr, Mr Geoffrey Rippon, Mr Paul Channon, Mr Nicholas Scott and Mr Peter Thomas. If such action led to fears that the shadow cabinet was about to be transformed into a Diehard debating society, they were unfounded. While the Thatcher leadership saw the arrival of Diehards like Mr Angus Maude, Mr John Biffen, Mr Teddy Taylor and Dr Rhodes Boyson to shadow cabinet and front bench positions, Ditchers were not seriously downgraded. The Ditcher flag was waved by Mr James Prior, Sir Ian Gilmour, Lord Hailsham, Mr Reginald Maudling, Mr Mark Carlisle and Mr Douglas Hurd. It is true that Sir Ian Gilmour was in a sense restricted from flag waving by being moved from shadowing home affairs to defence, and that his fellow Ditchers Mr Maudling and Mr Timothy Raison were dismissed by Mrs Thatcher, but the Diehard contingent did not emerge dominant. There were several reasons for this. First, Mrs Thatcher resisted the temptation to appoint the Diehard Sir Keith Joseph to the shadow chancellorship. In addition the white hope of the Diehard dinner tables, Mr John Biffen, failed to reconcile himself with the exposure associated with shadow cabinet status and his resignation in March 1977 robbed the Diehard[...] an astute and weighty exponent. While Mr Biffen later retur[...] shadow cabinet with responsibility for small businesses he[...] disappointment to those who had expected a more iconocla[...] tribution. Last, some of the Diehards that Mrs Thatcher did[...] such as Mr Winston Churchill and Dr Rhodes Boyson, were considered by their colleagues in the parliamentary party to be essentially politicians of the second (or third) eleven. By contrast non-Diehards like Mr William Whitelaw and Lord Carrington made less noise but remained at the centre of affairs very much as they had done under Mr Heath. In general, if Mr Heath created his leadership team in his own image, Mrs Thatcher was careful to avoid such an accusation. In this way she demonstrated her commitment to the re-establishment of that part of the traditional form of conversation in Conservative politics from which Mr Heath had departed.

Another example of Mrs Thatcher's attempts to restore a part of the traditional form of Conservative conversation neglected by Mr Heath was the effort she made to be an accessible party leader. Mr Airey Neave pointed out that after being elected leader, Mrs Thatcher told Conservative MPs that she would always be ready to talk and even Ditchers conceded that she kept her word. For example, one member of Mr Heath's administration who was unsure whether Mr Heath knew who he was, pointed out that Mrs Thatcher knew the name of every Conservative MP and was likely to know about each of their personal circumstances.[49] Another Conservative MP pointed out that 'She (Mrs Thatcher) has not made Ted's mistake of being inaccessible', and Mr Robert McCrindle, the MP for Brentwood and Ongar, noted that Mrs Thatcher paid some attention to those who sat behind her which was 'not an experience we are entirely used to'.[50]

Apart from bringing greater accessibility to the Conservative leadership, Mrs Thatcher was also responsible for an upturn in morale in the party in the country and in Parliament. Her declared aim of winning hearts as well as minds applied as much to her own supporters as to likely converts. Her private office acted on the assumption that as she performed more naturally 'in the flesh' than on television, the more she could get about the country the better.[51] Party members responded to her informality and concern in a way they had not responded to Mr Heath, and although there were complaints that Mrs Thatcher talked too much on the constituency rounds, her ability to elicit tears of emotion from many representatives at the 1975 annual conference following her set piece speech was a sign that within her own party she struck a sympathetic chord. Morale in the parliamentary party improved immeasurably too. In part the state of morale in the House was determined by the variable political situation. In the autumn of 1976 and the spring of 1977, for example, Conservative MPs felt as if they had the wind in their sails and were in a state of vague euphoria as they awaited the fall of the Government. By January 1978 this enthusiasm had evaporated and Conservative MPs, believing that they had missed their chance of office, were 'frustrated as hell . . . people sit around in gloomy groups, snarling and sniping'.[52] In general however, the melancholy that was evident in the parliamentary party after March 1974 did not return and under Mrs Thatcher's leadership the party as a whole seemed to take on a new impetus.

The fourth important change brought about by Mrs Thatcher concerned central-local relations in Conservative politics. While there was no great change in the aims the centre pursued in its relationship with the local associations, the means deployed to achieve these aims were altered. In this respect Mrs Thatcher acted in response to claims made in the leadership election that too much power had accrued to Central Office. First, the scheme to employ agents from the centre, which some Diehards had looked upon with grim foreboding, was quietly pigeonholed. It was argued that central funds were not available for the scheme, and that the burden imposed on constituencies to find money to pay their own agents was a valuable motivation for local revenue raising.[53] Second, there was a deliberate attempt to diminish the possibilities for 'empire building' which some Diehards claimed had taken place in Central Office with Mr Heath's consent after 1971. Although Sara Morrison resigned as party vice-chairman following the 1975 leadership election contest, Mr Heath's director-general, Mr Michael Wolff, remained. His dismissal by Mrs Thatcher in 1975 was regarded by Diehards as necessary to demonstrate the break with the old era. The concern to guard against the undue accretion of power in the party machine also manifested itself in the slightly reduced role given to the new director of organisation appointed in 1976 and to the vice-chairmen of the party appointed by Mrs Thatcher.[54] Last, greater parliamentary control was exerted in the Smith Square headquarters of Central Office than had existed in the past. Here, Lord Thorneycroft was very important and, after early bouts of ill health, he physically presided at Smith Square where those before him had sometimes only hovered. The early retirement (in 1976) of Sir Richard Webster, the director of organisation, was probably a reflection of this greater control, and of the concomitant decreased discretion which career officials were given under the new régime. Sir Richard's departure elicited howls of anguish from members of the National Society of Conservative and Unionist Agents who complained in their journal that increased control by Mrs Thatcher's political 'henchmen' was a threat to their profession. The vituperativeness of the attack by the agents on the 'disastrously insensitive and devious' actions of Lord Thorneycroft reflects the decline in morale in the party machine following the financial cuts and the extent to which (in the words of one Conservative MP) Lord Thorneycroft had acted to 'cut them (Central Office) back a peg or two'.[55] Those who considered that Lord Thorneycroft had departed this early life had clearly to think again!

Notes

1   Cosgrave, *Margaret Thatcher: a Tory and Her Party*, 1978, pp 197, 219.

2   Complaints about conference management were made in *Set the Party Free*, GLYC, 1969; economic policy motion proposed by Hooson, *Conference Handbook*, 1978, p.34.

3   Tebbit, *CCVR*, 1977, p.39; motion proposed by Brown, *CCVR*, 1977, p.34.

4   Interview with Conservative MP, 12 January 1978.

5   Interview with CTU national official, 10 January 1978.

6   Silvester MP, quoted in *The Manchester Evening News*, 24 October 1977; interview with Conservative MP, 12 January 1978.

7   Interview with shadow minister, 20 January 1978; interview with shadow minister, 15 February 1978.

8   Interview with shadow minister, 15 February 1978.

9   Conservatives bestowed the epithet 'poor' upon anyone defeated by a Scottish Nationalist in a general election. Mr Campbell lost Moray and Nairn to the SNP in February 1974, and afterwards became Baron Campbell of Croy; interview with shadow minister, 16 February 1978; interview with shadow minister, 20 January 1978.

10   Interview with shadow minister, 20 January 1978.

11   *The Daily Telegraph*, 22 January 1976; interview with shadow minister, 20 January 1978; interview with shadow minister, 16 February 1978; interview with Conservative MP, 8 June 1976; interview with shadow minister, 20 January 1978; on Heath policy groups see King, 'How the Conservatives evolve policies', *New Society*, 20 July 1972.

12   Young, 'The Iron Lady rides out from Finchley', *The Sunday Times*, 3 October 1976; interview with shadow minister, 20 January 1978; Lewis, 'Where is the body of Conservatism?', *The Daily Telegraph*, 11 February 1976; Lambton, 'Time for the Tories to drop their petty differences', *The Times*, 17 January 1976.

13   Lambton, ibid.; interview with Scottish Conservative MP, 20 October 1976; interview with Conservative MP, 27 January 1978; for a criticism of Heath, see Bell, quoted in Dalyell, *Devolution: the End of Britain?*, 1977, pp 159-60.

14   Seyd, 'Case study: democracy within the Conservative party?', *Government and Opposition*, 1975, pp 222-4, 225, 229-31, 233.
15   'You, gentle reader, may think that the attempt to impose a Parliamentary control over public expenditure in Britain is an Everest of a task. Mountains are for climbing.' Du Cann, *Parliament and the Purse Strings*, 1977, p.23.
16   Morrison, 'Remaking the party machine', *Crossbow*, October 1973, pp 10-11.
17   Interview with Central Office official, 25 September 1978.
18   Kohler, 'Blue-black: the Conservatives and the ethnic minorities', *The Conservative Agent's Journal*, August 1978.
19   Conservative and Unionist Central Office, *Annual Report*, 1975/76; 1978 *Conference Handbook*, p.174.
20   Behrens, 'Blinkers for the carthorse: the Conservative party and the trade unions, 1974-1978', *The Political Quarterly*, 1978, pp 457-73.
21   Interview with Central Office official, 25 September 1978; Hardman to Conservative trade unionists, Bradford, 11 March 1978.
22   Note by the party treasurers, *Income and Expenditure Account of the Central Funds of the Conservative and Unionist Party for year ended 31 March 1974* (Hereafter *Accounts* to 31 March 1974); note by the chairman, deputy chairman and party treasurers, *Accounts* to 31 March 1975; ibid.
23   *Accounts* to 31 March 1975; *Conservative and Unionist Central Office Annual Report*, 1975/76 (Hereafter *Annual Report*, 1975/76); ibid., 1976/77, 1977/78; Thorneycroft, *CCVR*, 1975; *The Daily Telegraph*, 2 November 1975.
24   *Accounts* to 31 March, 1971/75; *Annual Report* 1975/76; Thorneycroft, *CCVR*, 1975; *Conservative Agent's Journal*, September 1975.
25   *Link Up with the Conservatives: Fund Raising Events*, CCO, 1976; *Annual Reports* 1976/77, 1977/78.
26   Rose, *The Problem of Party Government*, 1974, p.224; *Labour Research*, September 1977; *Annual Report*, 1975/76.
27   For business contributions to Conservative funds between 1974 and 1978, see *Labour Research*, August 1975 and 1976; and 19 September 1977 and 1978; for European referendum contributions, see Labour party research department, *Information Paper no.5*, September 1975.
28   'Tories fear city and industry may back Liberals', *The Daily Telegraph*, 17 September 1975.
29   Macmillan quoted in Sampson, *Macmillan: a Study in Ambiguity* (1967), 1968, p.48; for contributions by type of company see *Labour Research*, August 1976, September 1977/78; for contributions in 1973 and 1974 see *Labour Research*, March 1974, August 1975.

30   For donations by company between 1973 and 1978 see *Labour Research*, March 1974; August 1975/76, September 1977/78.

31   For Diehard criticism of Heath's use of advertising men see Butt, in Boyson (ed.) *1985*, 1975, p.94; Morrow, 'Image maker behind Mrs Thatcher's growing assurance', *The Daily Telegraph*, 3 October 1975; Crowder, 'The Margaret Thatcher look', *Woman's Own*, (sic) 31 January 1976.

32   *Accounts* to 31 March 1975; *Annual Reports*, 1975/76, 1976/77, 1977/78; interview with Conservative MP, 12 January 1978.

33   Foster, 'Tories pick Saatchi', *Campaign*, 31 March 1978; Foster, 'How Saatchi plans to sell the Tories', *Campaign*, 7 April 1978; *Campaign*, 11 August 1978; ibid., 4 August 1978.

34   Benn, quoted in *Campaign*, 4 August 1978; Healey, ibid., 26 May 1978; Rees, quoted in *The Guardian*, 7 September 1978.

35   Fowler, quoted in *The Times*, 11 October 1978; Thorneycroft, quoted in *Campaign*, 16 June 1978.

36   Interview with member of Thatcher's private office, 17 November 1976.

37   McCrindle, quoted in *The Times*, 14 May 1976; Fairburn, quoted in *The Daily Telegraph*, 6 September 1976.

38   Eyres (Selsdon Group), quoted in *The Daily Telegraph*, 12 February 1976; Gordon, quoted in *The Sunday Telegraph*, 10 October 1976; for critical motions see *Conference Handbook*, 1976, motion 602, p.124; ibid., 1977, motions 1380 and 1385, p.176; Central Council *Meeting Handbook*, 1977, pp 24-5.

39   Peyton, quoted in *The Times*, 22 May 1976; interview with Conservative MP, 12 January 1978; interview with Conservative MP, 27 October 1976; interview with Conservative MP, 8 June 1976; interview with Conservative whip, 26 February 1976.

40   Howe, 'In search of stability', *The Daily Telegraph*, 26 January 1976.

41   Butler, Baker, Brittan, Goodhart, Alison (eds) *One Nation at Work*, 1976, pp 14-15; *The Right Approach to the Economy*, 1977, p.49.

42   McNair-Wilson, letters, *The Daily Telegraph*, 25 May 1976.

43   Gilmour, *Inside Right*, 1977, p.140; Hurd, quoted in *The Daily Telegraph*, 24 May 1976.

44   Griffiths, *Fighting for the Life of Freedom*, 1977, p.13; Howell, *Time to Move On*, 1976, p.6.

45   Thatcher, *CCVR*, 1975; Thatcher, CCO *News Service*, 8 October 1976; Thatcher, *CCVR*, 1975.

46   Thatcher, *CCVR*, 1977; Thatcher, CCO *News Service*, 8 October 1976.

47   Thatcher, *CCVR*, 1977; Thatcher, CCO *News Service*, 8 October 1976.

48   Interview with shadow minister, 15 February 1978; interview with Conservative MP, 27 January 1978.

49   Neave, quoted in Murray, *Margaret Thatcher*, 1978, p.128; interview with shadow minister, 20 January 1978.

50   Interview with Conservative MP, 27 January 1978; McCrindle, quoted in *The Times*, 28 June 1976.

51   Interview with member of Thatcher's private office, 17 November 1976.

52   Interview with Lancashire Conservative party official, 31 August 1977; interview with Conservative MP, 27 October 1976; interview with Conservative MP, 27 January 1978.

53   Interview with senior Central Office official, 25 September 1978; *The Conservative Agent's Journal*, September 1977.

54   Interview with member of Thatcher's private office, 17 November 1976; interview with a Conservative party vice-chairman, 26 February 1976; interview with senior Central Office official, 25 September 1978.

55   Interview with senior Central Office official, 25 September 1978; 'Off with their heads', *The Conservative Agent's Journal*, February/March 1976, p.3; interview with Conservative MP, 12 January 1978.

5 Conservative economic policy

> 'If the British electorate was invited to share in the denunciations of corporatist tendencies by Mrs Thatcher and Sir Keith Joseph after 1974, then the student of politics is entitled to ask why neither of these politicians saw fit to resign in the face of what Diehards called corporatist tendencies before 1974.'

One of the most crucial problems that Mrs Thatcher's Conservative party had to confront concerned economic policy. This was crucial for at least two reasons. First, because it involved a consideration of Conservative relationships with the trade unions which had been the Achiles heel of the 1970 Conservative Government. The confrontation with the miners in 1973 and 1974 had after all preceded (and probably precipitated) a general election which ousted the Conservatives from office in 1974. Second, the problem involved taking a stand on the role of government in society and on the principal causes of inflation. It was over these issues that the Diehards and the Ditchers were in gravest dispute. This chapter displays the tension that existed between Diehard and Ditcher economic prescriptions. It demonstrates that under Mrs Thatcher Conservative policy was etched around the liberal and Diehard faith in the market mechanism and the clear distinction between economics and politics. Ditchers were more equivocal about market mechanisms and less clear in their distinction between politics and economics. Diehards and Ditchers came together however in their determination to make the trade union movement more representative.

In chapter 2 we saw that Diehards stressed the overriding importance of reducing the Government's role in society. This position was rooted in economic and moral considerations. The economic arguments were that excessive government activity caused inflation because it involved the creation of new money and deficit financing, and that the market had its own metabolism which was well able to regulate activity. The unrestricted atmosphere of freedom permitted by the market made possible innovation, it stimulated efficiency and it facilitated higher productivity. The moral argument was that a Conservative believed in individual freedom and potentiality when he was not a creature of the

69

...iehard assertions legitimised a Conservative economic
...   Mrs Thatcher that was directed towards monetarism,
...   ilic spending and direct taxation. They also legitimised a
...   of the State's role in wage bargaining and in business
...   s in the private sector. Only in these ways could the individual
...   uely enfranchised and gain the responsibility, self respect and
'... ust independence' which freedom brought.[1]

At the core of Diehard economics lay monetarism. The term
monetarist had in common with the epithet 'whig' an element of
uncertainty. Whereas whigs had in common rebel ancestors and a plenti-
ful supply of money, monetarism was more concerned with the money
supply. Sir Keith Joseph explained that to be a monetarist was to
believe that the rate of increase in the supply of money must be
steadily decreased until it matched the increase in production. This
was a necessary but not sufficient condition of sound economic
management, and should be complemented by strict control of the
size of government borrowing and a reduction in the State's share of
the nation's resources.[2] Given its perceived importance, it is unsurprising that monetarism should have become a central feature of
Conservative policy statements during Mrs Thatcher's leadership. In
1976 monetary policy was 'vital', a year later it had a 'key' role while
in 1979 it was 'essential'. Indeed, the homily contained in *The Right
Approach to the Economy* (1977) that the management of money was
a necessary but not sufficient recipe for economic rectitude was lifted
almost verbatim from Sir Keith Joseph's Preston speech of September
1974.[3]

To the Diehards a necessary concomitant of monetarism was cutting
public expenditure and reducing direct taxation. The cuts in the public
sector borrowing requirement of £3,500 million by the Labour
chancellor in 1977 did nothing to dampen their enthusiasm for spending cuts. Indeed, outside the 'untouchable' area of law and order and
defence, they vied with each other to produce ways of cutting and
controlling expenditure. Mr Russell Lewis and Dr Boyson called for
wholesale denationalisation, Mr Nicholas Ridley advocated a winding
up of the health service and the creation of a new system altogether
free of state monopoly, and Sir Keith Joseph joined with Mr John
Biffen in calling for a cessation of poisonous subsidies to business and
industry.[4] As far as controlling expenditure was concerned Mr Iain
Sproat proposed to 'clean up' the social security system to prevent
waste as a result of fraud or claims contrary to natural justice, and
Mr Edward du Cann, from his position as chairman of the Public
Accounts Committee campaigned hard to extend the financial control of the House of Commons over the executive.[5]

Official policy statements sympathised with the spirit of this

Diehard analysis. In 1976 *The Right Approach* maintained that public spending cuts were essential to bring the economy back into balance, to avoid an explosion in the money supply and an acceleration of the rise in prices. As output had fallen since 1973 and Labour spending plans had risen, 'very large reductions' would be unavoidable. This would probably involve reductions in the scale of some public services.[6] *The Conservative Manifesto 1979* emphasised the need for such 'substantial economies' though *The Right Approach to the Economy* (1977) noted that cuts were to be annually progressive and certainly not indiscriminate.[7] However, all the documents were hazy about what cuts would be involved. *The Right Approach* for example, argued that as long as the prospects for the economy were obscure, precision was not possible. Priority for cuts centred around two areas. The first included 'expensive Socialist programmes' such as the nationalisation of building land, and government intervention in industry particularly that of the National Enterprise Board. Indiscriminate housing subsidies also came into this category. The second area of savings involved the elimination of what Conservatives called waste, extravagance and bureaucracy. Economies would be looked for in the operation of the tax and social security systems, direct labour schemes, and the unspecified duplication between central and local authorities. The reduction of State spending would be assisted by the imposition of rigorous cash limits for the total annual expenditure of government programmes.[8] This vagueness was exploited by the Labour party during the 1979 general election campaign and prompted an attempt by the shadow chancellor, Sir Geoffrey Howe, to illustrate how a careful reading of the reports of the Public Accounts Committee revealed a host of specific ways in which waste could be eliminated.[9]

For the Diehards, tax cutting appeared to be an article of faith. Taxes should be cut for two reasons. First, because such action would act as an incentive for the liberation of energies by companies through investment and by citizens through effort. According to Sir Keith Joseph, it was disastrous that wealth-creating entrepreneurs and managers — the 'ulcer' people — had been rewarded for their labours with the highest marginal tax rates in the free world, together with abuse, discouragement and interference.[10] Second, as private property was an essential bulwark of freedom, Conservatives should enable more people to save out of earnings and to pass their savings onto their heirs.[11] Conservative policy statements agreed that tax cuts acted as a liberation of energies. The 1979 manifesto asserted that to become more prosperous Britain had to be more productive and the British people given more incentive.[12] Each of the policy statements envisaged a reduction of the rates of direct taxation for everyone and an 'enterprise package' of tax reforms designed to restore incentives to save, invest and work hard. In 1977, for example, *The Right Approach to the Economy* asserted that the burden of income tax would be reduced throughout the scale, that capital transfer tax was to be transformed by cutting rates and extending relief, and that capital gains tax was to be adapted so that only true (and not paper) profits were subject to tax. Conservatives would have no truck with a wealth tax and question marks were also raised about the investment income surcharge. These points were reiterated in less detail in the 1979 manifesto. The Conservatives conceded that such tax cuts would have to be financed in part by a switch to indirect taxation.[13] Once again however, the Labour party complained that the Conservative proposals were entirely unclear, and Mrs Thatcher was driven to respond that her party could not be more specific until they had seen the Treasury 'books'.

The Diehards viewed the prospect of an incomes policy with little relish: it involved a mincing up of everything that was dear to them. Four reservations about a statutory or rigid incomes policy were voiced, and these were directed not only at the supporters of incomes policy in general, but at the Labour Government's own anti-inflation programme as it developed from 1974. First, an incomes policy was said to be corporatist in its effects, in that it took decision making away from elected representatives in Parliament. By way of illustration, Mrs Thatcher said that the Labour Government's social contract involved a handful of trade union leaders dictating to the Government the level of public spending and the number of industries to be nationalised. This usurped the functions of Parliament. Mrs Thatcher told the 1976 Conservative annual conference that Parliament was the only body which represented all the people, and democracy was not government of, by and for a section of the people but of by and for *all* the people. Her conclusion was that 'If a trade union leader . . . wants to run the country he or she should stand for Parliament'.[14] Second, incomes policy deflected union leaders from their legitimate, traditional and essential economic role, which Mrs Thatcher considered was to represent and bargain for their members at work.[15] Once they were deprived of this role (through the operation of incomes policy pay guidelines and limits) union leaders were bound to take an active interest in more obviously political matters like outlining what should be the general level of state spending. Third, incomes policies were said to be economically inefficient. Mr Nicholas Ridley pointed out that they caused grave damage to production which was largely stimulated by higher pay. They also involved an erosion of differentials and the building of a dam of resentment caused by the suppression of wage demands.[16] To the Diehards this last point was uncontrovertably demonstrated by the dislocation manifest throughout the winter of 1978 when lorry drivers and a variety of public servants refused to settle within the Government's 5 per cent pay limit. Last, Mrs Thatcher claimed that a statutory policy put the state in confrontation with major sectional interests in society. When unions disputed the maximum permitted rise in wages they had no alternative but to confront the Government, which had persuaded Parliament to authorise the maximum.[17] Here, those Diehards who had supported Mr Heath in the confrontation with the miners in 1974 were making a public declaration that they would not make the same mistake again.

Most of these arguments found their way into party policy statements,[18] and these in turn counselled a return to what the 1979 manifesto called realistic and responsible pay bargaining.[19] This meant several things. There would be no narrow and exclusive deals which bypassed Parliament. The Government would 'give some conclusions' about pay increases for the 3½ million employees in the public sector because it had a duty to control public spending.[20] However, it would approach the matter having set limits for the rate of growth of money supply, government borrowing and the state's share of the nation's resources. These would be applied with 'firm and unshakeable resolve', and the establishment of cash limits would put a ceiling on public sector wages. In the private sector however, responsibility in pay bargaining could not be defined by the Government setting a fixed percentage for everyone since circumstances were different in each enterprise. As Mrs Thatcher explained, 'If you are to have good industrial relations, people who do well should naturally expect to have more pay'. And if the Government were to permit freedom to bargain they could not then rescue with someone else's money those who had bargained themselves out of the market.[21] The Diehard road to freedom was not without its chilling winds.

Ditchers responded to these policies in ways varying from the expression of cautious and conditional approval to the voicing of contempt for the alleged simplicity of the strategy. As far as monetary policy was concerned, Ditchers did not reject it as an important economic tool. Mr Nicholas Scott of the Tory Reform Group wrote that sound finance was the only foundation upon which prosperity could be based and that it was not just a Diehard plot to deny social progress.[22] Nevertheless, Ditchers were worried that some Diehards saw monetary policy as 'some automatic mechanism' which turned economics into a natural science.[23] From within the shadow cabinet Sir Ian Gilmour warned that no single economic doctrine gave a complete explanation of economic behaviour and that eclecticism was essential. From the outside, Mr Peter Walker appeared to stress that this point had not been heeded by complaining that the shadow cabinet's fascination with monetary policy diverted them from exposing the failures of the Labour Government.[24]

The Ditchers also instilled some notes of caution to the debate on cutting public expenditure. They did not deny that some aspects of state spending like welfare provision or housing subsidies had gone too far or that spending could be tempered by increased efficiency in government.[25] However, as they began their analysis from the position that decisive state action was necessary and sometimes even productive, to them root and branch cuts in public spending were in general either undesirable or unfeasible. (The one area of exception was housing. From 1975 Mr Peter Walker strongly pushed the idea of transferring the entire council housing stock to existing tenants.)[26] They believed that state programmes to alleviate poverty and create jobs went a long way to foster a sense of community in society. In any case, as Mr Walker pointed out, it was naive to suppose that net public spending was cut by abandoning road or house building schemes when such programmes created employment and thereby saved expenditure on unemployment pay and social security benefits.[27] Furthermore, much of the public sector, like the coal, electricity and gas industries, was essentially productive and the consequences were deleterious when it was deprived of investment. Some Ditchers even conceded that the logic of this position was to countenance *increased* public spending in areas other than (and in addition to) law and order and defence. In any event, all Ditchers agreed that to bring spending into balance was a complicated task and could not be achieved merely by a stroke of the pen and the burning of incense at the graveside of Adam Smith.[28]

There was substantial consensus between Ditchers and Diehards on the need to cut taxes and so provide incentives for wealth creation.[29] (This unity was hinted at by praise in *The Right Approach* for the attempt by the Heath government to introduce a radical programme of tax reform. Considering that policy statements after 1975 read as if Conservative history had come to a conclusion with the years of Conservative government in the 1950s, this was a significant acknowledgement.) However, unanimity was harder to find on the matter of incomes policy. Ditchers agreed that incomes policy, either statutorily enforced or voluntarily induced in return for a social contract had many potential or actual disadvantages. They acknowledged that it might usurp the function of Parliament by providing an opportunity for trade union leaders to enter into negotiation with government as socialist politicians. The result of this might indeed be to tie the hands of unions to government and deflect union leaders from their function of speaking out freely for their members. Furthermore, they agreed that incomes policy eroded differentials and that it introduced politics into wage negotiations by putting the Government behind management who were trying to stick to the limits. Nevertheless, despite these concessions to Diehard argument, Ditchers considered that intervention by the state through some form of incomes policy in both the public and private sectors could not be avoided. Certainly in the public sector it was vital that the Government must have a view about what its employees should be paid. Much of the public sector consisted of monopoly and social service which suspended the discipline of the market.[30]

The root of Ditcher scepticism however, lay in their inability to be as optimistic as the Diehards about the possibility of the market generating equitable solutions for the private sector. Mr James Prior, for instance, told the 1978 Conservative annual conference that he sometimes envied those whose faith was totally in the free market mechanism.[31] The market had too many imperfections. In the first place its equilibrium was unhinged by union monopoly power which operated in the key areas of the economy. One Ditcher pointed out that where competition was distorted by monopoly of this kind, the theory of the market demanded that the monopoly should be broken up or supervised and controlled. Market economists should therefore seek to abolish trade unions or accept an incomes policy.[32] Next, a return to 'free collective bargaining' in the market involved a restoration of traditional bargaining procedures. According to Mr Prior these were not vehicles for efficiency, but an inefficient, complex and irrational web of relationships resulting in leap-frogging claims in total disregard of profitability and output. This suggested that free collective bargaining was a jungle, and a recipe for what Mr Heath called massive inflation.[33] Third, Ditchers argued that it was impossible to divorce the private from the public sector. Mr Heath, for example, asked Lancashire miners in a rhetorical fashion what would happen if a government tried to hold down wages in the public sector while private sector wage increases continued apace. Not only would public sector workers not accept such differential treatment, but the British public, thinking that 'nothing is worse than unfairness would immediately come to the side of those in the public services'.[34] As a result, Mr James Prior told a Monday Club fringe meeting at the 1978 annual conference, that a Conservative Government would have serious difficulties in attempting to allow freedom to private firms in pay bargaining while seeking to impose absolute restraint in the public sector. The lesson to be drawn from experience, Mr Heath concluded, was that the private sector could not be entirely dissociated from what happened in government-controlled public sector pay negotiations.[35]

The Ditchers therefore saw the necessity for intervention by the state, but they disagreed amongst themselves about the precise nature of that intervention. Some Ditchers favoured the reintroduction of a statutory policy for an indefinite period.[36] Others considered that this would put Britain on the road to a corporate state but thought that as a temporary expedient a statutory policy was a better way of combat-ting inflation than having a free for all in wage claims.[37] Mr Heath denied that it was Conservative heresy to be in favour of an incomes policy. He argued that unless a pay norm was specified no one would know what the country could afford. Furthermore the norm had to be binding because if it was labelled 'take it or leave it' people would leave it. For these reasons a Conservative Government might well have to have some form of pay control if it came to power, and there would certainly be a need for an independent board to settle problem cases of relativity under an incomes policy. For good measure Mr Heath added that there were a large number of people in the shadow cabinet who believed an incomes policy had got a part to play.[38] One Ditcher shadow minister who publicly entertained the possibility of a statutory policy was Mr James Prior. In October 1978 he pointed to the danger of unemployment rising under a future Conservative Government committed to monetarism. In those circumstances a statutory policy might become necessary.[39] While Mr Prior conceded that after three years of rigid pay policy under the Labour Government the time had come for greater flexibility both he and Sir Ian Gilmour helped to ensure that party policy statements resisted the Diehard temptation of flatly and permanently ruling out a statutory policy.[40]

This rearguard action aside, Mr Prior's main contribution to the incomes policy debate centred around his advocacy of what was called 'concerted action'. What Mr Prior meant by the term was the creation of a forum where Government consulted with the major economic interests about the implications of fiscal and monetary policies for pay bargaining and unemployment. This might be linked to Parliament through a reform of the select committee system.[41] Concerted action found its way into Conservative policy statements. *The Right Approach to the Economy*, for example, suggested that the National Economic Development Council might be the most appropriate forum for consul-tations, and that it might have contacts with the general subcommittee of the House of Commons select committee on expenditure.[42] The proposal had strong support from Ditchers. They had long tinkered with the idea of an assembly of industry, linked to Parliament and drawn from all sections of industrial life, which would help to create a new climate of economic co-operation.[43] Further, they believed that intense consultation between Government, industry and trade unions was vital for sound economic management.[44] By contrast, Diehards looked upon the suggestion with extreme unease. Mr John Biffen was worried and Sir Keith Joseph was 'nervous' about the danger that public pronouncements on any expected increase in total income would be translated into a minimum figure for collective bargaining. Mr Biffen therefore thought that concerted action of this kind should only have a modest role to play, and both Sir Keith Joseph and Mrs Thatcher omitted to refer to it in important speeches on economic policy.[45]

There are several avenues of enquiry to be pursued in consideration of this Conservative economic policy that was presented to the electorate in 1979. The first concerns the designation of the political role of trade unions as non-legitimate and the supposed disjunction between politics and economics. First, it is not only tempting but it also appears reasonable to suggest that there was a large amount of 'do as I say' rather than 'do as I do' about the Conservative concern to proscribe the political role of trade unions. Whereas the Conservatives in opposition after 1974 denigrated the idea of narrow and exclusive deals because they undermined the supremacy of Parliament and dragged the unions into the political arena, the Heath administration in fact conducted tripartite talks with the TUC and CBI about counter-inflation legislation. Indeed Mr Edward Heath described his discussions with the CBI and TUC in October 1972 as 'an offer to employers and unions to share fully with the Government the benefits and obligations involved in running the national economy'. Many Diehards argued then, and subsequently that the whole ethos of this strategy was, in the words of Mr John Biffen, 'designed to diminish the authority of Parliament', or following Mr Hugh Fraser, an essentially cabalistic strategy pointing towards a semi-corporate state.[46] Leading Conservatives in Mrs Thatcher's shadow cabinet including Mrs Thatcher herself, Sir Keith Joseph and Sir Geoffrey Howe were each collectively responsible for this policy between 1972 and 1974 yet chose not to disassociate themselves from it by resignation from the cabinet. If the British electorate was invited to share in the denunciations of corporatist tendencies by Mrs Thatcher and Sir Keith Joseph after 1974, then the student of politics is entitled to ask why neither of these politicians saw fit to resign in the face of what Diehards called corporatist tendencies before 1974.

Second, Conservative policy statements and Diehard speeches after 1974 suggested that distinguishing between the political field and the economic was easy. In reality distinguishing between the political and economic activities of trade unions is a complex business: the border changes because it is in part determined by government policy, and hard to discern because it is in part contingent upon an interpretation of union motive. Two examples will illustrate this. The 1970-74 Conservative Government extended the boundary of the political considerably. They took responsibility for defining maximum increases in wages through counter-inflation legislation. They therefore defined as *political* an attempt by the miners to achieve through strike action increases outside of the maximum. For most of the miners however, the strike was simply a matter of *economics* (we want more pay) yet the

Government accused them of defying Parliament and placing themselves beyond the pale of the Constitution. As Mr Enoch Powell explained in November 1973, 'the greater evil still of all counter-inflation policies is the antagonism, at once futile and disastrous, which they inevitably set up between the state on one side and the various classes and interests in the community on the other side'.[47] If the February 1974 general election was about whether the miners strike was political, and at the time Conservatives certainly argued that this *was* what the election was about, then the verdict of the electorate was certainly not an overwhelming endorsement of Conservative definitions of the political activity of trade unions. Irrespective of the result of the 1979 general election this hesitancy from the electorate might have been expected to induce some caution from Conservatives in distinguishing between politics and economics. Instead, Conservative literature emphasised the supposed dichotomy between politics and economics by dressing up the political activity of unionists as unscrupulous and underhand. In the real world however, even where there is no statutory incomes policy to extend the boundary of the political, it is very hard to know when 'politically motivated militants' can fairly be said to be acting now politically and now economically. Given a situation of inflation and wage restraint under the Labour Government followed by a Conservative election victory, one Conservative postulated 'there will be so much pent-up frustration among ordinary workers that a Marxist union leader will find it very easy to stir up disruption and strikes for a "fair wage".' The question·this Conservative then directed himself to concerned the way in which a future Conservative administration would deal with this 'political' threat. But is this a political issue or is it an economic one? While Conservative activists complained that policy statements contained nothing substantial about *how* the Conservatives would deal with a political confrontation by the unions, the problem of distinguishing *what* constitutes a political confrontation did not enjoy any kind of substantial analysis by Conservatives before the 1979 election.[48]

The third avenue of exploration involves a discussion of what ramifications Conservative policy had for their relations with the trade unions. This was a most important matter if only because the questions 'How will you deal with the unions? Can you govern?' were invoked more frequently than almost any other after the Conservatives were removed from office in 1974. The Conservative leadership offered an assurance that they would listen to what union leaders had to say, without embarking on any special relationship. Because a very large element of union members would be supporters of a Conservative Government and because the most influential leaders could be relied upon to co-operate with a Government of any party, the idea that unions would not co-operate with a Conservative Government was what Mr James Prior called 'a gross calumny on virtually all their members'.[49]

Having established that they expected to be able to work with union leaders the Conservatives set about devising strategies to confront and eradicate what they saw as the overtly political aspects of union activity. If Diehards and Ditchers quarrelled over public spending and incomes policies, many of them were at least united over how to deal with a political challenge by a union to a Conservative Government and over their long term aspirations for trade unions. The Conservatives affirmed first, that a direct political challenge to a newly elected Conservative Government would be resisted 'firmly and decisively'. (In a well publicised secret report prepared for Mrs Thatcher in Spring 1978, Lord Carrington pointed to the difficulties that a future Conservative Government would have in defeating powerful trade unions in a direct confrontation.) Second, they affirmed that if the law of the land was broken it had to be enforced.[50] This was generally understood to mean that rather than acquiesce in a political strike the Conservatives would call a general election. Matters were somewhat confused by Mrs Thatcher's suggestion in September 1977 that instead of an election the Conservatives might hold a referendum. This, she later said, had a very respectable Conservative history. The status of this proposal was unclear, as it may well have been a piece of kite flying to divert attention from shadow cabinet squabbles over the Scarman Report on Grunwick (see chapter 6). In any event it has certainly been argued, not least by Conservatives, that holding a referendum lies in uneasy harmony with a policy which otherwise claimed to be concerned about the supremacy of Parliament.[51]

In the medium and long term, Conservative policy to neutralise the political activity of unions was to make them more 'representative'. Institutionally, Conservative policy remained broadly the same despite the change in party leadership. Impetus for the reform of union procedures was to come from within the union movement itself, but the Government would provide public funds for the election by secret ballot of union leaders.[52] Elections might even be held in the workplace rather than in what Mrs Thatcher called 'the spooky upstairs room after the last bus has gone'. After 1975 there was also a sustained attempt to encourage more people to participate in union affairs. At the 1975 party conference Mr Tom Ham, a long time Conservative trade unionist made a notable contribution by berating the party for letting the number of Conservative trade union organisers dwindle, and rounding on Conference representatives for not attending union meetings. Mrs Thatcher echoed this theme by calling on Conservative electors and 'all our supporters in industry' to 'go out and join in the work of your unions. Go to their meetings, stay to the end, and learn the union rules as well as the far Left knows them'.[53]

Attempts to encourage this on a systematic basis centred on the re-formation of the Conservative Trade Unionists' (CTU) Department at Conservative Central Office, under the direction of Mr John Bowis. The lack of contact between the Conservative party and trade unions in the postwar period (described in chapter 4) did little to enhance under-standing of trade unions in the party. Conservative trade unionists were either treated with condescension — 'the chap who says a few sweet words in a "gor blimey" accent and gets a standing ovation for it' — or hostility. As Mr Prior told Conservative trade unionists in Bradford, 'It sometimes takes a bit of guts to go to Conservative meet-ings and say you are a Conservative trade unionist'.[54]

Because of the bedrock of hostility to unions within the Conservative party, there were suspicions that the CTU was revitalised to infiltrate and destroy the trade union movement. As the chairman of the Cleveland and Whitby CTU freely admitted, 'there are some short-sighted members of our party who would be pleased to see this happen'. This motive however was denied by CTU officials who pointed out that one of their three aims was to improve communication and understanding between the Conservative party and the unions. With regard to promoting understanding, the CTU believed that there was a large educative process which needed to be conducted. As Mr Fred Hardman, the CTU national committee chairman put it, in the inaugural issue of *CTU News*:

> Within the Party our grass-roots are anxious to see something done about the unions. This feeling is there wherever I go. It is indes-tructable . . . *We have the task of educating our Party to the facts of life* . . . We have got to show that unions are democratic organi-sations and the most effective way is to use the democratic processes (within unions) to achieve our aim of changing the image of the unions.[55]

The CTU also made a big attempt to improve communication bet-ween the Conservative party and the unions by improving the quality and flow of information within the party about trade union affairs. The CTU department of Central Office saw itself as a channel between the parliamentary party at one end, and the shop floor at the other. It periodically briefed Conservative members of Parliament through the post. Information was collected on such matters as union finances, union democracy, and picketing, by dispatching questionnaires to CTU members. Returns were then analysed and the findings dissemi-nated.[56] There were also five specialist CTU groups, which fed data into the parliamentary party, and the party in general. These covered the areas of national government, public services, teachers, the post office and the ASTMS union. The groups had reached various stages of development by 1979. The post office group, for example, met for the first time only on All Fools Day 1978. Each of the groups had a parliamentary 'link man', and each appeared to function largely in London, though their organisers hoped that as they became established they would become more national.

The second aim of CTU was to begin to change the character of the trade union movement itself. In part this was to be achieved by encouraging Conservatives to become involved in union activity. For a party which had a declared intention of depoliticising unions this may seem to have been a somewhat incongruous aspiration. Indeed, there were some people in the CBI (Confederation of British Industries) who expressed concern that CTU activity might lead to the setting up of Conservative cells in their factories, and thus to the further politicisation of industrial relations. However, it was claimed that the intention was for Conservatives to behave as 'good unionists' rather than as political activists. In other words, Conservatives were encouraged to bargain hard to secure maximum benefits over such issues as conditions, pay, redundancies, hours and sickness benefits.[57] This differed from 'the disruptive objectives of the far Left' in that collective bargaining was not to be used to undermine profitability. Rather, maximum benefits could best be achieved by fostering the success of firms.[58]

Thus it was argued that a paradox existed in which although it was a *political* organisation, the Conservative party encouraged trade unionists to pay attention to what were seen to be *economic* issues. The CTU would not therefore lead to the further politicisation of industrial relations. How convincing an argument was this? In the first place, by 1979 the CTU was in such an early stage of redevelopment that its effect on industrial relations was very marginal. (It is difficult to give accurate figures for membership of the CTU because there was no central record file. However, even though Central Office encouraged constituencies to set up CTU groups, many local parties appeared to be short of people to organise them.) Second, while the CTU earnestly sought to divorce politics from economics in industrial relations, the very fact that its organisational base was within Conservative Central Office coloured reactions to it from other trade unionists. For instance, when the CTU department issued a list of 'moderates' who should be supported in the CPSA (civil servants) union elections, Mr Kendall, the union general secretary, accused the Conservative party of political interference. While this particular controversy served the purpose of putting the CTU in the public view for the first time ('Kendall in fact launched us') it served to illustrate how the CTU could be viewed as a small group of politically motivated men. On the other hand, the incident may have escalated because (in this particular case) the CTU department's method of compiling the list and the manner in which it sent it out were neither discrete nor accurate. (The list of moderates appears to have been drawn from the International Socialist source, *Redder Tape*.) Indeed, some trade union leaders, rather than being suspicious of its political complexion expressed the view that once the CTU developed, Conservatives could 'stop belly-aching (about the unions) and get in there'.[59] However, as the third aim of the CTU was to bring 'good unionists' into the Conservative party, whatever the CTU did to encourage unionists to opt out of paying the political levy to the Labour party, the logic of the organisation seems to have condoned party political recruitment on the factory floor. If there was to be recruitment for the Conservative party, then why not for the Socialist Workers party?

In conclusion several observations appear to be pertinent. First, under Mrs Thatcher, Conservative economic policy took on a liberal and Diehard flavour with its emphasis on the importance of the market, monetarism, public spending cuts and cash limits. Ditchers acquiesced in parts of this policy though they had grave reservations about putting so much trust in the market mechanism. Their dissent was most clearly voiced over incomes policy, and it is worth noting that in the end Conservative eschewal of incomes policy under Mrs Thatcher was significantly less explicit than the utter rejection of it by Mr Heath in 1970.

Second, the Diehard attack on what was seen as the political activity of trade unions took place against a background of Mr Heath's interventionism between 1972 and 1974. Sir Keith Joseph, Mrs Thatcher and Sir Geoffrey Howe bore collective responsibility for this policy and did not speak out against it. Their reasons for acquiescence could not have been on the grounds that they were not aware of the arguments against intervention since Mr Enoch Powell, Mr John Biffen and many other Diehards articulated the 'dangers' of the Heath 'corporatist' strategy at the time. The almost wholesale adoption of these arguments by Sir Keith Joseph and Mrs Thatcher once they left office in 1974 was, at the least, ironical and must have been rather galling to those who had bathed in the solitude of monetarism through the years of the Heath Government. The irony is compounded by two historical circumstances. Some of the waste, extravagance and bureaucracy which the Conservatives promised in 1979 to sweep away had been ushered in through institutional reforms brought about by Conservatives themselves after 1970, e.g. the reform of local government. (To Mr John Biffen it was 'folly', to Lord Blake it was 'peculiarly disastrous', while Mr Russell Fairgrieve used a more indelicate expression at a 1976 party conference fringe meeting on decentralisation.)[60] However, the reorganisation of the National Health Service by Sir Keith Joseph towers above all other examples, not the least because it stands as testimony to the spectacular transformation of his opinions after 1974. In addition, however firm and unshakeable was the resolve of Conservatives in the 1979 general election to keep the money supply under control, certain of the more realistic Diehards like Mr John Biffen were bold enough to concede that the Labour Government elected in 1974 established a better control over money supply 'than for some years past'. In the solitude of their tents, without an election husting in sight, Diehards could reflect that 'for some years past' perhaps included the years of Conservative Government in 1972 and 1973.[61]

Last there were clearly some problems about the Conservative distinctions between politics and economics. This was most graphically illustrated in the activities of the CTU department which set out with the apparently conflicting ambitions of depoliticising the union movement and encouraging unionists to join the Conservative party. The conundrum is laid bare by reference to the genius of Conservatism as ideology and its ability to describe what the other parties do as political, but to pose actions by Conservatives as simply 'common sense' and not political at all. This was a valuable propaganda myth, but a myth which Conservatives themselves appear to have swallowed whole.

Notes

1   Joseph, *Reversing the Trend*, 1975, p.20; Joseph, *The Business of Business*, 1977, p.3; Thatcher, 'Is it really worth going on in small business?', *Conservative Monthly News*, February 1978; Thatcher, Glasgow, quoted in *Conservative Monthly News*, February 1978.
2   Joseph, *Reversing the Trend*, 1975, p.31; Joseph, *Monetarism is Not Enough*, 1976.
3   *The Right Approach*, 1976, p.8; *The Right Approach to the Economy*, 1977, p.8; *The Conservative Manifesto 1979*, p.8; *The Right Approach to the Economy*, p.14.
4   Lewis, 'Denationalisation' in Boyson (ed.), *1985: An Escape from Orwell's 1984*, 1975, pp 19-28; Boyson, *Centre Forward*, 1978, p.86; Ridley, *Social Service Sense*, 1977; Joseph, *The Business of Business*, 1977, p.7; Biffen, *Political Office or Political Power?*, 1977, p.4.
5   Sproat, 'How to clean up social security', *Conservative News*, February 1978; Du Cann, *Parliament and the Purse Strings*, 1977, p.23.
6   *The Right Approach*, 1976, pp 24, 25.
7   *The Conservative Manifesto 1979*, p.8; *The Right Approach to the Economy*, 1977, p.10.

8 *The Right Approach*, 1976, p.25; *The Conservative Manifesto 1979*, p.9; *The Right Approach to the Economy*, 1977, p.11; *The Right Approach*, 1976, p.25; *The Conservative Manifesto 1979*, p.9; *The Right Approach to the Economy*, 1977, pp 11, 12.

9 Howe, Oxted, April 1979, Conservative research department, *Daily Notes*, 18 April 1979, pp 52-7.

10 Joseph, 'Fair deal for the job-makers', *Conservative Monthly News*, May 1975.

11 Maude, 'The path that leads to freedom', *Conservative Monthly News*, September 1975.

12 *The Conservative Manifesto 1979*, p.10.

13 *The Right Approach*, 1976, pp 41-2; *The Right Approach to the Economy*, 1977, pp 26, 31; *The Conservative Manifesto 1979*, pp 13, 14; *The Right Approach to the Economy*, 1977, p.27.

14 Thatcher, *CCVR*, 1976, p.139.

15 Thatcher, quoted in *The Guardian*, 10 January 1978.

16 Ridley, MP 'Why do we want stage III pay curbs anyway?', *Conservative Monthly News*, May 1977.

17 Thatcher, Wrexham, quoted in Cosgrave, *Margaret Thatcher: a Tory and Her Party*, 1978, p.214.

18 *The Right Approach to the Economy*, 1977, pp 13, 19; *The Right Approach*, 1976, p.37.

19 *The Conservative Manifesto 1979*, p.11.

20 *The Right Approach to the Economy*, 1977, pp 15-16, 20.

21 Howe, *CCVR*, 1978; Joseph, ibid.; Thatcher, ibid.; Thatcher, quoted in *The Times*, 11 October 1978.

22 Scott, MP, *The Cambridge Reformer*, October 1977.

23 Carr, quoted in *The Guardian*, 20 February 1975.

24 Gilmour, *Inside Right*, 1977, p.232; Walker, MP, quoted in *The Times*, 19 January 1976.

25 Gilmour, op.cit., pp 152, 154; Waldegrave, *The Binding of Leviathan*, 1978, p.46.

26 Walker, *The Ascent of Britain*, 1977, pp 163-76.

27 The editors talk to Peter Walker, MP, *The Cambridge Reformer*, October 1977, pp 10-11.

28 Walker to Tory Reform Group, quoted in *The Guardian*, 13 October 1977; Russel, *The Tory Party: its Policies, Divisions and Future*, 1978, p.34.

29 Walker, 'Targets for the 1980s', *Conservative Monthly News*, November 1977; Carr, 'Why our industry is in such trouble', *Conservative Monthly News* February 1975; Prior, quoted in *Conservative News*, July 1978.

30 Prior, *CCVR*, 1976, p.55; Prior, *CCVR*, 1978, quoted in *The Times*, 11 October 1978; Heath, *Hansard*, 7 July 1976, col.1423;

Walker, *The Ascent of Britain*, 1977, p.68; Waldegrave, op.cit., pp 68, 70.

31 Prior, *CCVR*, 1978, quoted in *The Times*, 11 October 1978.

32 Carr, 'Incomes policy', *The Political Quarterly*, 1975, pp 403-4.

33 Prior, 'Consult the people', *The Guardian*, 14 December 1977; Gilmour, op.cit., p.235; Heath, quoted in *The Times*, 12 October 1978.

34 Heath, quoted in *The Guardian*, 31 October 1978; Heath, ibid., 8 October 1978.

35 Prior, quoted in *The Guardian*, 13 October 1978; Heath, *CCVR*, 1978, quoted in *The Times*, 12 October 1978.

36 Carr, 'Incomes policy', *The Political Quarterly*, 1975, p.408.

37 Walker, *The Ascent of Britain*, 1977, p.68.

38 Heath, Chelsea, quoted in *The Times*, 20 October 1978; Heath, quoted in *The Times*, 30 October 1978; Heath, quoted in *The Guardian*, 9 October 1978; Heath, quoted in *The Guardian*, 31 October 1978.

39 Prior, quoted in *The Guardian*, 9 October 1978.

40 Prior, *CCVR*, 1978, quoted in *The Times*, 11 October 1978; *The Right Approach*, 1976, p.37, does not rule out a statutory policy and *The Conservative Manifesto 1979* fails to mention the possibility. For Maudling's attempts to discuss incomes policy at shadow cabinet, see *Memoirs*, 1978, pp 208-9.

41 Prior, 'Consult the People', *The Guardian*, 14 December 1977; Prior to CTU annual conference, 11 March 1978.

42 *The Right Approach to the Economy*, 1977, pp 16-17.

43 Walker, *The Ascent of Britain*, 1977, p.81; Gilmour, op.cit., p.249.

44 Heath, *Hansard*, 7 July 1976, col. 1411-2.

45 Biffen, op.cit., pp 16-17; Joseph, quoted in *The Times*, 13 October 1978.

46 Heath, quoted in Boyson, *Centre Forward*, 1978, p.34; Biffen, 'Painful need to re-state attitudes', *The Sunday Times*, 27 October 1974; Fraser, 'Tories need a new leader . . . ', *The Times*, 31 January 1975.

47 Powell, quoted in Wood, 'Mr Powell questions mental stability of Prime Minister', *The Times*, 30 November 1973.

48 Clarke (Bow Group). Open letter to Thatcher, quoted in *The Times*, 5 October 1976; Landa, 'Sorry to be ungrateful', *The Brighton Reformer*, October 1976.

49 Prior, *CCVR*, 1976, pp 54, 55; Thatcher, *Conservative Monthly News*, April 1976; *The Right Approach to the Economy*, 1977, p.20; Prior, *CCVR*, 1977.

50 *The Times*, 18 April 1978; *The Right Approach to the Economy*, 1977, p.21.

51 Higgins, MP, letters, *The Times*, 21 September 1977.
52 *Putting Britain First*, 1974, p.12; *The Conservative Manifesto 1979*, p.11.
53 Thatcher, *CCVR*, 1976, p.56; Ham, *CCVR*, 1975; Thatcher, *CCVR*, 1975.
54 Kirk, *CCVR*, 1976, p.52; Prior, CTU annual conference, Bradford, 11 March 1978.
55 Shotliff, *Conservative Monthly News*, May 1977; Hardman, 'Message from the Chairman', *CTU News*, March 1978 (Author's italics).
56 Interview with CTU national official, 10 January 1978.
57 Ibid.; *CTU News*, March 1978.
58 Interview with CTU national official, 10 January 1978; Prior, *Conservative Monthly News*, May 1977; Prior, CCO *News Service*, 615/76, 16 June 1976.
59 Interview with CTU national official, 10 January 1978.
60 Biffen, *Political Office or Political Power?*, 1977, p.21; Blake, *Conservatism in an Age of Revolution*, 1976, p.20.
61 Powell in Ritchie (ed.) *Enoch Powell: a Nation or No Nation? Six Years in British Politics*, 1978, pp 13-30, 82-91; Blake, op.cit., pp 20-1; Biffen, op.cit., p.14.

6 The Conservative party, Grunwick and the closed shop

> 'Mr Prior did not see the matter in quite this light. First, he was "irritated, even more" by what he saw as Sir Keith's attack on the judicial system. Second, he was "obviously displeased" at what he understood to be Sir Keith Joseph's meddling in a functional area beyond his responsibilities. "The unions know," he maintained, "that *I* speak on behalf of my colleagues in the shadow cabinet and the parliamentary party on these matters".'

This chapter discusses Conservative attitudes to trade unions and employment law. It examines Diehard and Ditcher views about trade unions, and shows how certain Diehards could reasonably be said to be hostile to trade unions. In displaying Conservative policy on employment law it is argued that under Mrs Thatcher the Conservative party was as equally disposed to acquiesce in positions favoured by the TUC as it had been under the leadership of Mr Heath after February 1974. This acquiescence provoked a campaign by Diehards within and on the fringe of the party against what they saw as the appeasement of trade union power. In this respect Mr James Prior the shadow employment spokesman came in for special criticism. Ditchers responded with vigour and the result was tension and division within the Conservative party over the emotive issues of the closed shop and the Grunwick dispute. Given the extent of the industrial discord and the attendant impatience with strikers in the winter of 1978 and the spring of 1979, it is argued that the continued Conservative party policy of acquiescence was all the more surprising.

Mrs Thatcher told the annual conference of the CTU in 1976 that it was 'one of the most absurd myths of our national and political life' that the Conservative party was hostile to trade unions.[1] A careful assessment of Diehard strictures on the malevolences of trade unionism calls this into question. Certainly, on rare occasions Diehards were heard defending unions. For example Mrs Thatcher reminded the CTU annual conference that more successful western nations than Britain had strong trade unions, so they could not be blamed for all the country's ills.[2] In general however, Diehards were extremely critical of many aspects of trade union behaviour. They distinguished between the rank and file union members — 'decent, law-abiding, patriotic people' (good) — and the TUC establishment — 'tasting and enjoying immense political power' through association with the Labour Government (bad).[3] To some Diehards these leaders were literally tinpot Marxist gauleiters, adopting Hitlerite tactics and producing revolutionary circumstances in Britain.[4]

The Diehard critique of trade unions focussed on what were understood to be their monopoly powers to distort market mechanisms and control prices. In the first place, unions depressed living standards and reduced employment by holding back productivity. They used their strength to impose overmanning, and so reduce the investment that would otherwise have taken place. This kept real pay low, costs high and therefore markets smaller than they would otherwise have been. Sir Keith Joseph noted that in this respect union leaders and workers were more intransigent than their colleagues in north west Europe.[5] Second, by artificially restricting the supply of labour, through operation of the closed shop, unions might have raised the wages of particular groups of workers above the level they would have reached in a free market, but with disastrous consequences. These higher wages were gained at the expense of those who were excluded from employment. Any increased demand for products was absorbed by an increase of the wages of the workers already employed rather than by an influx of additional workers. Furthermore, the corollary of restricting the supply of labour was to undermine individual freedom to decide whether one wanted to join an association or not. Under closed shop agreements workers were given the choice of union membership or unemployment.[6]

Diehard prescriptions for these problems varied. Some of the more robust Diehards appeared to see little useful role for trade unions in a free society. They believed that what their opponents called 'bashing the unions' was indeed the task that lay before the Conservative party,[7] and remarked ominously that while trade unions might once have served a noble purpose 'memories of Trafalgar do not lead to demands that the navy should again use wooden ships'.[8] Others were at pains to emphasise that trade unions were an indispensable and immensely valuable asset in a democratic society, and one of the economic counterparts of political freedom. All of them, however, appeared to believe that union power should be reduced, because the imbalance of power between unions and management barred the way to national recovery. In terms of immediate political programme this involved action to outlaw the closed shop, steps to limit the powers of picketing, stopping the payment of supplementary benefits to the families of strikers, and the repeal of large sections of employment law enacted after 1974.[9]

While the Ditchers often articulated the same grievances against the trade unions, they could be distinguished from the Diehards in their explanation for trade union behaviour. The allegedly erroneous political and economic attitudes of union leaders were understandable in that they were the price the Conservatives paid for the prejudices created by an era of socially irresponsible capitalism.[10] Modern day industrial conflict had been created by the attitudes of the nineteenth century and 'the Puritan ethic of work' in which the fittest survived and most of the rest went to the wall. In consequence, conflict inevitably became endemic in our society 'and as we all know British traditions die hard'. Tactically the logic of this position was that caution was necessary, especially following the debacle of the Industrial Relations Act. As Mr James Prior advised, trade unions were a powerful body present in everyday life, and Conservatives had to learn to understand this and try to come to terms with them.[11]

These not always harmonious attitudes structured the debate in the Conservative party about employment law. Employment law is like the Holy Roman Empire — it is hard to fully comprehend, but also very important. Because it is a complex subject, it is easily open to misinterpretation, either intentional or not. An examination of employment law shows that it was simplistic to suggest, notwithstanding the comments by Mr James Callaghan and Mr Michael Foot during the 1979 general election campaign, that the position of the Labour Government was to keep the law out of industrial relations. The Employment Protection Act, for example, indicated a marked new determination by the trade union movement to achieve their ends by legislation rather than by collective bargaining.[12] It was, as one Labour MP candidly conceded, 'our version of the Industrial Relations Act',[13] and in the second reading debate Conservatives were not slow to point out the irony that Labour members had been 'shouting loud and long that the law and lawyers should be kept out of industrial relations. Yet in this Bill they seek to introduce the most extensive and detailed code of special laws we have ever seen'.[14] Further, although the Trade Union and Labour Relations Act 1974 and the Trade Union and Labour Relations (Amendment) Act 1976 broadened trade union immunities within the law, they also provided, for the first time, positive statutory support for the closed shop.[15] A major reason for this legislative approach was that while the Labour party made a song and dance about repealing the Industrial Relations Act, and while the Conservative party pledged in October 1974 not to reintroduce it,[16] the post-1974 Labour Government wanted to re-enact and to some extent extend the many legislative provisions in the 1971 Act relating to unfair dismissal. This being the case, the concomitant was to define what constituted a closed shop, because under a closed shop an employee could be 'fairly' dismissed for not belonging to a union.[17] The supposed dichotomy of post-1971 Conservative legalism and post-1974 Labour non-legalism was therefore false.

As part of this new legalism, the Labour Government in 1974 succeeded in passing through Parliament what became the Trade Union and Labour Relations Act. This reintroduced certain trade union immunities in law (concerning restraint of trade, trade disputes and vicarious liability) and provided a statutory basis for the closed shop. Section 6 subjected union rules to certain legal requirements covering items like funds, elections and disciplinary action, while section 5 provided a remedy against arbitrary or unreasonable exclusion (or expulsion) from unions. The remedy was a declaration from an industrial tribunal, followed if necessary by enforcement through the High Court. The 1974 Act also confirmed picketing as 'not unlawful'. Picketing was defined as the attendance of persons at or near somebody's place of occupation, or anywhere else that somebody was, except his home. In general the protection of section 15 was given if certain conditions were met. First, the attendance had to be in contemplation or furtherance of a trade dispute. Next the sole purpose of attendance had to involve the communication of information or the persuasion of somebody not to work. Last the attendance had to be peaceful. (If section 15 is not available, mere attendance by a picket may be a civil law nuisance.) Section 13 of the Act provided that an act in contemplation or furtherance of a trade dispute was not actionable in tort if it induced another person to break a contract of employment.[18] In their attempt to secure the prospect of industrial peace (and no doubt also to win the October 1974 general election), the Conservatives accepted this Act, as amended by Parliament, as the basis of future employment law.[19]

After the second general election of 1974 however, the Labour Government, temporarily unrestrained by its minority status, introduced further measures to extract those provisions which the Conservatives had regarded as sensible amendments to the 1974 Act. By 1976, after the long delayed passage of the Trade Union and Labour Relations (Amendment) Act, and the Employment Protection Act, the industrial settlement seemed to be far closer to the position aimed for by the TUC.[20] Under the Amendment Act, sections 5 and 6 of the 1974 Act were repealed. This removed the obligation for union rules to conform to mandatory requirements (apart from union accounts and superannuation) and abolished the statutory recourse to a tribunal and the High Court. In place of the tribunal, the TUC persuaded affiliated unions to establish their own machinery for dealing with appeals by members against union executive action. They recommended that the appeals machinery should have an independent element. The TUC also appointed what it called an independent review committee to consider appeals from individuals who were dismissed from or refused entry to a union where a closed shop existed. In addition, the definition of a trade dispute was widened and the law on the closed shop altered considerably. Under the 1974 Act, the dismissal of an employee had been regarded as fair where a closed shop agreement existed, and the employee refused to join or stay in a union specified by the agreement or 'another appropriate independent trade union'. There were two exceptions to this: first where the employee objected on grounds of religious belief, and second where 'on any reasonable grounds' the employee objected to membership. Under the amending legislation, reasonable grounds of objection were removed and the concept of an appropriate independent trade union replaced by a union specified by the closed shop agreement. This meant that unions and management could now state without question to which union the employee must belong.[21] Last, the law relating to picketing was changed. Section 3 of the 1976 Act made it lawful not only to induce breaches of a contract of employment, but also breaches of any contract, including commercial ones. According to the Conservative law spokesman, Mr Leon Brittan MP, the effect of this was often to legalise the picketing of deliveries by firms which were not involved in the industrial dispute which precipitated the picketing.[22]

Clearly then, acquiescence by Mr Heath in the industrial settlement of 1974 was not the same as acquiescence in the revised settlement reached by 1976. As Conservative MP Mr Kenneth Baker argued, 'My colleagues and I contend that, taken with two or three other measures which are now before Parliament, it (the Employment Protection Bill) substantially increases the influence status and power of organised trade unions'.[23] What was the Conservative response under Mrs Thatcher to the erosion of the 1974 settlement? To have called for a *repeal* of all those measures which eroded the 1974 settlement would have left the Conservative party in the same position which it adopted under Mr Heath. Party policy statements did call for a restoration of the 1974 position in the politically sensitive areas of the closed shop and picketing, but in other areas they called for rather less.

In *The Right Approach to the Economy* (1977) the Conservative party called for 'satisfactory voluntary arrangements' to be incorporated into a code of practice to restore (broadly speaking) the 1974 position with regard to the closed shop, and to restore the remedies against exclusion or expulsion from a union. If these voluntary arrangements did not provide adequate safeguards for individuals, then legislation was promised. However, the Conservatives took advantage of the industrial dislocation of the winter of 1978-79 to pledge to restore the 1974 closed shop and union exclusion or expulsion arrangements by a change in the law. Satisfactory voluntary arrangements were no longer enough. In addition, the Conservatives proposed that closed shop agreements should be drawn up only if an overwhelming majority of the workers involved voted for it by secret ballot. This procedure would be contained in a statutory code under section 6 of the 1975 Employment Protection Act.[24] The reluctance to legislate against the closed shop itself came in the wake of consistent Conservative characterisation of it as an 'undoubted encroachment on freedom of choice'.[25] After 1974 however, Conservatives became increasingly aware that a change in law was not an automatic guarantee of a change in behaviour. As Mr Prior explained to the 1977 annual conference of the National Union of Conservative and Unionist Associations, 'The truth is . . . that even under that (Industrial Relations) Act, setting out as it did to ban the closed shop, arrangements continued to exist under the counter, and because they were not open, some of the abuse and unfairness they created were unfortunately more difficult to deal with'.[26]

On picketing, the 1979 manifesto declared that 'we believe' that picketing rights should be limited to those in dispute picketing at their own place of work. The implementation of such a proposal would have undone the provisions of the 1974 Act which permitted picketing in places other than the place of work. Taking however the natural construction of the words, an expression of belief was less than a commitment to action.[27] (To be scrupulous it should be recorded that the paragraph on picketing was concluded with the portentous declaration that 'we shall also make any further changes that are necessary so that a citizen's right to work and go about his or her lawful business free from intimidation or obstruction is guaranteed'.) The 1979 manifesto also announced that 'we shall ensure that the protection of the law is available to those not concerned in the dispute but who at present can suffer severely from secondary action'.[28] This followed Mrs Thatcher's call in January 1979 for legislation against 'secondary picketing'. While the law made no distinction between primary and secondary picketing, according to Mr Callaghan the 'plain man' could distinguish between primary picketing which was intended to stop the 'blackleg' from doing the work of the man on strike, and secondary picketing which was intended to stop another worker from pursing his normal occupation.[29] In the view of the Attorney-General, Mr Silkin, and in the light of judgements from the High Court[30] *a certain amount* of secondary picketing was clearly not illegal under the 1974 Act. In this sense the proposal to ban secondary picketing could be viewed as an attack on the 1974 settlement. Nevertheless, the 1979 manifesto referred only to 'such amendment as may be appropriate of the 1976 legislation in this field'. The reasonable assumption to be drawn from that statement was that the 1974 picketing settlement would be left intact.[31]

Concerning other changes from the 1974 settlement, Conservatives were studiously vague. They pledged amendment to laws 'such as the Employment Protection Act where they damage . . . business . . . and actually prevent the creation of jobs'. Near the top of the list was a review of the terms of reference for the Advisory, Conciliation and Arbitration Service set up under the 1976 Act. These terms of reference gave ACAS the generalised duty of encouraging the extension of collective bargaining which meant that it was thought unlikely to be neutral in particular recognition disputes between employers and unions. In consequence, for many trade unionists, ACAS was a body which held out the prospect of the unionisation of small companies in Britain. The terms of reference also permitted unions and not employers to submit recognition disputes to ACAS, which according to Mr Prior was 'unfair and indefensible' and may well have resulted in employers not wishing to use ACAS and not having a great deal of confidence in it.[32] Significantly however, certain other important changes made in 1975 and 1976 appear to have been acquiesced in. Most notable was the acceptance of ACAS itself. Although some industrial writers noted that ACAS as constituted was the quintessence of corporatism, and although Conservative policy statements after 1974 warned of the dangers of corporatism to the democratic process, the Conservatives showed no readiness to abolish it if they were returned to power. Indeed, in committee they attempted to rid the council of its three academic members on the grounds that they did not come from either side of industry. As Mr Barney Hayhoe explained: 'I am not all that happy with the thought that, if the legislation goes through, there would always be these three slightly 'odd bods'. I do not mean odd in their abilities, but in the sense that they do not come from one of the constituencies of either employers . . . or trade unions and the TUC'. A deletion on these lines would have *added* to the corporate character of ACAS. There also appeared to be acquiescence in the widening of the definition of the term trade dispute and in the abolition of statutory controls over union rules.[33]

It might be argued that this acquiescence was offset by the commitment in 1979 to change the law on the payment of social security benefits to the families of strikers, and kite flying on the need to negotiate no strike agreements in the public utilities. Mr Prior noted that the timing of the legislation on strike pay would require full discussions with unions and 'other people'. The aim was for unions to accept a share of the responsibility for the welfare of the families of men who went on strike. The Conservatives would assume that union strike pay was about £9 a week, and would give unions time to build

up their strike funds. However, it is important to note that this proposal was basically a repetition of one made by the Conservatives under
Mr Heath in the October 1974 general election, and fell considerably
short of the Conservative threat in February 1974 to cut off benefits to
strikers altogether.[34] In summation, it seems plausible to argue that
after 1974 Conservative policy was no less accommodating to trade
unions in the area of employment law under Mrs Thatcher than it
had been under Mr Heath. The general policy of accommodation, which
was largely identified with Mr Prior, the shadow employment spokesman, caused a large amount of irritation within the Conservative party
at every level. Dissenting Diehard voices were raised against the general
drift of (what was called) Mr Prior's policy, more specifically against
Conservative policy on the closed shop and the Grunwick dispute, and
against Mr Prior himself.

James Prior as Marshal Petain

Attacks on Mr Prior's policy were very vigorous. For the National
Association of Freedom for example, Conservative policy was akin to
running up the white flag to see if anyone would salute, while the
Selsdon Group called it 'one of the greatest sell-outs to trade union
power'.[35] The attacks also tended to employ analogies between contemporary Conservative industrial policy and policies of appeasement
common in the 1930s. So for the Diehard Mr Norman Tebbit, unnamed
Ditchers in the party had 'the morality of Laval and Petain . . . The
doctrine of appeasement is still to be heard'.[36] Similarly, for Mr Robert
Moss writing in *The Free Nation*, official Conservative pragmatism was
on a par with collaboration with Hitler Germany,[37] while a leader in
The Daily Telegraph warned that 'reasonable' men like Mr Prior and
Neville Chamberlain were sometimes too liable to attribute their own
virtues to those with whom they had to deal.[38]

Moving from the general to the specific, a sustained attack was
launched against the decision not to legislate against the closed shop.
The bulk of the onslaught was orchestrated by the National Association
for Freedom (NAFF). For NAFF, the law giving positive statutory
support to the closed shop was 'the cruellest, most discriminatory and
nastiest piece of legislation since 1945'.[39] To aid and draw attention to
those workers 'fairly' dismissed because of their reluctance to join a
union, marches and rallies were held, a Workers in Freedom Fund was
set up, and claims to the European Court of Human Rights at
Strasbourg were supported and encouraged. In addition, in 1976,
Mr Stephen Hastings, one of the Conservative MPs affiliated to NAFF,
tried to amend the Government's closed shop legislation, but his

attempt to introduce a Bill was defeated by 287 votes to 226.[40] The 'crunch' on the closed shop came at the 1977 Conservative annual conference at Blackpool. In the industrial relations debate Mr Prior won the backing of representatives for a speech in which he defended the official Conservative position that 'we are against the closed shop — full stop', but that for the moment outlawing legislation was not appropriate. (See above pp 47-8).

James Prior as Marshal Dillon

The second contentious issue was the Grunwick affair. On 20 August 1976 a go-slow in the mail order department at the Grunwick Processing Laboratories in Brent, precipitated a long running dispute. One man was dismissed, three or four others walked out, and one woman asked for her cards. By the end of 23 August 65 employees had come out on strike and the next day about 60 of these strikers joined APEX (Association of Professional, Executive, Clerical and Computer Staff), which declared the strike official on 31 August. Grunwick sent out dismissal notices to the strikers, now numbering 137, on 2 September.[41]

While few would dispute that these events took place in the order described, what the Grunwick affair actually concerned depended upon who one asked. For the union and the Labour party, the dispute was about union recognition and the reinstatement of workers sacked after protesting against conditions of employment 'which indigenous British workers and even immigrants who have been here for some time would never dream of accepting'.[42] For the company however, advised and assisted by the Diehard Mr John Gorst MP, and the National Association for Freedom, no 'real' grievances were ever put forward and the dispute stemmed from Grunwick exercising its legal right to dismiss employees for breaking their contracts of employment. From there it developed into a recognition dispute, totally unrelated to the original controversy, and it ended as a stand against what Grunwick and Diehards saw as the malevolencies of the corporate state.[43]

In the Conservative party there was agreement that the dispute concerned a union recognition question, but Conservatives thought that even more important was the threat to the rule of law. There was unanimity in the party that by selectively blacking Grunwick mail in November 1976 and June 1977, members of the Union of Post Office Workers (UPW) were deliberately breaking the law. There was also agreement that the Government was doing little or nothing to take sanctions against this action, or even to condemn it. Last, there was agreement that the mass picketing outside Grunwick had led to gross violation of the law, and should be stopped immediately.[44]

On the recognition issue however, the Conservative party was badly split, particularly in the shadow cabinet where Mr Prior admitted, somewhat euphemistically, that there were 'differences of emphasis' between himself and the Diehard Sir Keith Joseph. The problem took its character from two aspects of the industrial settlement established by the Labour Government in 1975. The first concerned the perceived objectivity of ACAS. Almost from the beginning, when ACAS offered its services to Grunwick in September 1976, the company was reluctant to co-operate because it questioned the likely fairness of an investigation by a body (ACAS) whose very purpose, according to section 1 of the Employment Protection Act, was to encourage the extension of collective bargaining. (Mr George Ward, the Grunwick managing director, complained of the lack of 'full impartiality' of ACAS, though he admitted that he was not aware of this at the beginning of the dispute when he simply thought arbitration superfluous.)[45] In the end ACAS went ahead without the co-operation of Grunwick, and recommended recognition of APEX. However, the second point is that under the Employment Protection Act, ACAS was not given power to *enforce* recognition on employers, for fear that any penalties for non-recognition might ignite a general movement in favour of similar legal constraints over the activities of trade unions.[46] There was thus no obvious way out of the dispute, and the last resort was a court of inquiry headed by Lord Justice Scarman, which published its findings on 25 August 1977. Scarman reported that 'The company, by dismissing all the strikers, refusing to consider the reinstatement of any of them, refusing to seek a negotiated settlement to the strike, and rejecting ACAS offers of conciliation, has acted within the letter, but outside the spirit of the law. Further, such action on the part of the company was unreasonable when judged by the norms of good industrial relations practice. The company has thus added to the bitterness of the dispute, and contributed to its development into a threat of civil disorder.'[47] Scarman recommended that the sacked workers be reinstated, that those not reinstated should be given ex gratia payments, and that APEX be recognised for the purposes of collective bargaining.[48]

There were markedly different responses to this from Ditchers and Diehards. Mr Prior had already said on 30 March 1977 that the ACAS report recommending recognition should be 'heeded'; and on 25 August he spoke in favour of a solution based on the Scarman inquiry's recommendations, negotiated by a mediator with the politicians keeping out of the dispute.[49] Sir Keith Joseph on the other hand attacked the Scarman court of inquiry and its findings at Hove on 1 September. In content, Sir Keith's attack bore a marked resemblance to the 'Counter-Scarman Report' issued by Grunwick in the wake of Scarman's findings. He first denigrated the use of the term court as 'a linguistic confidence trick'. A body with the word court in its name might have more chance of winning acceptance for what was essentially a political solution. Sir Keith then set about the Scarman findings. He claimed that the inquiry had been set up because of violence on the streets outside Grunwick, yet 'the industrial court scarcely refers to the violence which led to its own appointment, scarcely condemns the union under whose auspices the violence occurred'. The proper answer to violence on the street, he asserted, was the firm use of the existing law, or the form of the law, if the law was inadequate. Furthermore, Sir Keith maintained that Scarman's recommendations for Grunwick to reinstate the strikers, and recognise APEX were both objectionable. Reinstatement was objectionable because it did not take into account the attitudes of those workers who had not gone on strike, and recognition was inappropriate because it 'suggests the imposition beyond the dictates of the law of a union upon the staff of a company who have apparently overwhelmingly rejected both'. So for Sir Keith Joseph, Scarman's interpretation of reasonableness boiled down to accepting that 'the employer and the (non-striking) workers — the victims of illegality, violence and intimidation — should not only comply with the law but with the will of the law breakers'.[50]

Sir Keith's attack on Scarman was not lightly undertaken, especially as Lord Justice Scarman was a member of the judiciary whom he had held in high esteem. (Joseph cited Scarman's views with approval in *Freedom under the Law*, CPC, 1975, p.14.) However, the report's conclusions made it 'an imperative' that Sir Keith should intervene as he saw the rule of law threatened.[51] Reactions to his comments were mixed. The Ditcher Tory Reform Group for example, concluded that Sir Keith 'must be off his head', because they said that Scarman offered a solution which any sensible person would have accepted. Sir Keith should therefore be dismissed as shadow industry spokesman. Diehards however, could reasonably argue that Sir Keith's statement put him alongside them in their encouragement of Grunwick not to be 'bullied' into submission. In consequence, the National Association for Freedom who had assisted Grunwick in their legal battles against the postal 'blacking', and Mr Gorst MP, who had acted as adviser to Grunwick throughout the dispute, were delighted. The Diehard Selsdon Group was also pleased, and their secretary remarked that Conservatives who backed the Scarman report were guilty of capitulation to extreme union power. Mr George Ward (Grunwick managing director) and his 160 workers were fighting a battle the Conservatives should have identified with.[52]

Mr Prior did not see the matter in quite this light. First, he was 'irritated, even more' by what he saw as Sir Keith's attack on the judicial system. Second, he was 'obviously displeased' at what he understood to be Sir Keith Joseph's meddling in a functional area beyond his responsibilities.[53] 'The unions know', he maintained, 'that *I* speak on behalf of my colleagues in the shadow cabinet and the parliamentary party on these matters'.[54] This specific point was not denied by Sir Keith, who saw himself as speaking as a member of the public, with a consequent right to have his view heard.[55]

Mr Prior was therefore somewhat embattled. First he had been contradicted in an emphatic manner by a senior shadow colleague. As Mr Timothy Raison MP, a former colleague (dismissed by Mrs Thatcher) commented, it really was very difficult for a shadow spokesman in a particular field if his colleagues were not saying more or less the same thing as he was.[56] Second, his policy of accommodation, particularly with respect to the closed shop and Grunwick, was actively opposed and attacked within the party and on the fringe of it. Third, Mr Prior was subjected to verbal attacks on his own person. These were quite forceful, ranging from a description of him as having 'the sort of plummy acquiescent voice . . . passive and defeatist and yet oddly arrogant about the impossibility of reversing Labour measures' to a portrait which had him as a worshipper of expediency and a difference splitter who was forever seeking a compromise between right and wrong.[57]

Such attacks on Mr Prior and his policy did not help him in convincing trade union leaders of the seriousness of Conservative attempts at accommodation. As one CTU national official explained: 'Certainly our role is more difficult because of organisations such as the National Association for Freedom'. The public was led to believe that what was NAFF policy was in fact the party's policy. Yet in the face of all this strong vilification, Mr Prior emerged as 'a very strong character', apparently unmoved by the siren voices around him. Adopting the traditional demeanour of an Englishman in hostile surroundings, his upper lip remained resolutely stiffened.[58]

In conclusion, Conservative employment law policy showed a substantial amount of continuity between 1974 and 1979, notwithstanding the change of leadership. Given the strength of Diehard feeling about trade unions, and the seriousness of the industrial unrest in the winter of 1978-79, this is perhaps a little surprising. The Diehards in control of *Conservative News* devoted a great deal of space to the hardships caused by the winter of discontent. They wrote of manual workers who took 'guerilla' action and the 'humiliation' of manufacturers who went to plead with Transport and General Workers Union strike committees for 'permission' to move raw materials. A strike by a million public servants on 22 January 1979 became 'Black Monday', and the effect on hospital treatment and burials was recorded with great feeling.[59] The indignation caused by these activities was limited neither to Diehards, nor to members and supporters of the Conservative party. The Conservative leadership's response was to call for a change in the law on the closed shop and secondary picketing, for secret ballots in union elections and for no strike agreements in the public utilities. These proposals were a long way short of what many Diehards clamoured for. Above everything, the Thatcher leadership resisted yet again the temptation to outlaw the closed shop. This accommodation or hesitation can be interpreted in different ways. For some Diehards it was proof that Mrs Thatcher was being prevented from introducing robust policies because of 'idealess, rubberised' shadow colleagues.[60] For Conservatives suspicious of Mrs Thatcher's 'nineteenth century verities' however, it was comforting evidence that within the shadow cabinet, the Ditchers won some important battles, sometimes to the fury of Diehards on the backbenches.[61] For the student of politics perhaps the salient point is that many Conservatives were unlike the Bourbon rulers who were said to have learned nothing and forgotten nothing. Conservatives in the party leadership were determined to bend over backwards to prevent a replay of the confrontation between the trade union movement and the Heath administration. The ghost of the 1971 Industrial Relations Act haunted the meetings of the Thatcher shadow cabinet with considerable effect.

Notes

1   Thatcher, quoted in *Conservative Monthly News*, April 1976.
2   Thatcher, quoted in *Bradford Telegraph and Argus*, 11 March 1978.
3   Griffiths, *Fighting for the Life of Freedom*, CPC, 1977, p.9; Howell, *Time to Move On*, CPC, 1976, pp 19-20.
4   Buckmaster, 'Industrial progress or political anarchy', *Tory Challenge*, September 1977, p.5; Shenfield, 'What about the Trade Unions?', in Boyson (ed.) *1985: an Escape from Orwell's 1984*, 1975, p.32; Moss, 'Right to Work', *The Free Nation*, 28 May 1976.
5   Shenfield in Boyson, op.cit., pp 36-7; Joseph, 'Conditions for fuller employment', *The Right Angle: Three Studies in Conservatism*, 1979; ibid., p.27; Joseph, *Reversing the Trend*, 1975, p.8.
6   Hayek, 'The Powerful reasons for curbing union powers', *The Times*, 10 October 1978; Griffiths, op.cit., p.10.
7   Shenfield in Boyson, op.cit., pp 36-7.
8   Beloff, 'Tories: beware of the carthorse', *The Daily Telegraph*, 29 March 1976.
9   Griffiths, op.cit., p.9; Biffen, *Political Office or Political Power?*, 1977, p.18; Joseph, *Reversing the Trend*, 1975, p.53; Joseph, quoted in

The Daily Telegraph, 6 February 1979; Boyson, *Centre Forward*, 1978, pp 41-9, 73.

10   Walker, *The Ascent of Britain*, 1977, p.63.

11   Prior, CCO *News Service*, 615/76, 16 June 1976; Prior, quoted in *The Guardian*, 13 October 1978.

12   Benedictus, 'Employment protection: new institutions and trade union rights', *Industrial Law Journal*, 1976, p.23.

13   Rooker, *Hansard*, 28 April 1975, col.103.

14   Percival, ibid., col.114.

15   Weekes, 'Law and the practice of the closed shop', *Industrial Law Journal*, 1976, p.211.

16   *Putting Britain First*, 1974, p.12.

17   Weekes, op.cit., p.212.

18   Silkin, *Hansard*, 25 January 1979, col.707; Drake, 'The Trade Union and Labour Relations Act 1974', *Modern Law Review*, 1974, p.541.

19   *Putting Britain First*, p.12.

20   Drake, 'Recent legislation: old wine in new bottles', *Industrial Law Journal*, 1974, pp 344-40; on the delay over the Amendment Act, see Beloff, *Freedom Under Foot*, 1976.

21   Drake, 'The Trade Union and Labour Relations (Amendment) Bill', *Industrial Law Journal*, 1976, p.8; Weekes, op.cit., pp 220-1, and 218.

22   Brittan, quoted in *Conservative News*, March 1979.

23   Baker, *Hansard*, 28 April 1975, col.96.

24   *The Right Approach to the Economy*, 1977, pp 49-50; *The Conservative Manifesto*, 1979, p.10.

25   *A Strategy for Union Members*, CTU, 1976.

26   Prior, *CCVR*, 1977, p.40.

27   *The Conservative Manifesto*, 1979, p.10.

28   Ibid.

29   Thatcher, quoted in *The Guardian*, 18 January 1979; Callaghan, *Hansard*, 16 January 1979, col.1546.

30   United Biscuits (UK) Ltd *v* Fall. The case was brought by one of Mrs Thatcher's industrial advisers Sir Hector Laing. Mr James Prior was a United Biscuits board member. See *Industrial Relations Law Reports*, vol.8, no.3, March 1979.

31   Silkin, *Hansard*, 25 January 1976, col.707; *The Conservative Manifesto*, 1979, p.10.

32   Ibid., p.   ; Prior, Employment Protection Bill, Standing Committee F, *House of Commons Official Report*, 12 June 1975, 8th sitting, col.383; Prior, *Hansard*, 28 May 1975, col.55-6.

33   Rogaly, *Grunwick*, 1977, p.143; Hayhoe, Employment Protection Bill, Standing Committee F, *House of Commons Official Report*,

12 June 1975, 8th sitting.

34 *The Conservative Manifesto*, 1979, p.11; Prior, quoted in *The Guardian*, 12 April 1979; Prior, quoted in *The Daily Telegraph*, 12 April 1979; *Putting Britain First*, 1974, p.13.

35 *The Free Nation*, 15 October 1976; *The Sunday Telegraph*, 29 February 1976.

36 Tebbit MP, quoted in *The Guardian*, 13 September 1977. (Tebbit however, came round dramatically to back Prior at the 1977 annual conference.)

37 Moss, 'We must help this free man', *The Free Nation*, 30 April 1976.

38 'Living with the Unions', *The Daily Telegraph*, 12 October 1977.

39 Calcraft, 'Jimlet, or the art of giving Tories a bad name', *The Free Nation*, 9 July 1976.

40 *The Free Nation*, 25 June 1976.

41 Rogaly, *Grunwick*, 1977, pp 10-19, 171-2; *The Report of a Court of Inquiry under the Rt. Hon. Lord Justice Scarman OBE into a Dispute between Grunwick Processing Laboratores Limited and Members of the Association of Professional, Executive, Clerical and Computer Staff*, August 1977, Cmnd. 6922, (hereafter Scarman), para. 13, p.6, suggests that the precise number that walked out with Devshi Bhudia on 20 August is in doubt. Ward, *Fort Grunwick*, 1977, p.37, puts the number at 3.

42 Scarman, para.5, p.3; Urwin, *Hansard*, 4 November 1976, col. 1674. (See Davies, ibid., col.1680; and Pavitt, ibid., 30 June 1977, col.595.)

43 Ward, *Fort Grunwick*, 1977, p.42; Scarman, para.5, p.4; Gorst, *Hansard*, 30 June 1977, col.602; Ward, op.cit., p.46; ibid., pp 101-3.

44 Gorst, *Hansard*, 4 November 1976, col.1637; Walker-Smith, *Hansard*, 30 June 1977, col.590; Adley, ibid., 4 November 1976, col. 1643; Griffiths, ibid., 30 June 1977, col.625; Joseph, quoted in Ward, op.cit., p.73.

45 Ward, op.cit., pp 61-4.

46 Prior, quoted in *The Times*, 12 September 1977; Rogaly, op.cit., p.145; ibid., p.144.

47 Scarman report, para.67, p.22; para.72, p.22, defines 'unreasonably' as acting according to the letter, but not 'the spirit of the law'.

48 Scarman report, para.73, p.23.

49 Prior, quoted in Rogaly, op.cit., p.78; Prior, quoted by Grigg, 'Ward politics', *The Spectator*, 10 September 1977.

50 Ward, op.cit., pp 101-13; Joseph, quoted in Aitken, 'Joseph attacks the Scarman "Con" Trick', *The Guardian*, 2 September 1977; Joseph, letters, *The Times*, 12 September 1977.

51 Interview with shadow minister, 16 February 1978.

52   Aitken, 'Joseph attacked all round for defence of Grunwick', *The Guardian*, 3 September 1977; Aitken, 'Selsdon Group backs George Ward', *The Guardian*, 5 September 1977.

53   Interview with CTU national official, 10 January 1978.

54   Prior, quoted in Hoggart, 'Prior pushes Tory rift over unions into open', *The Guardian*, 12 September 1977. (Author's italics).

55   Interview with shadow minister, 16 February 1978.

56   Raison, 'Closed options', *The Guardian*, 11 October 1977.

57   Calcraft, 'Jimlet or the art of giving Tories a bad name', *The Free Nation*, 9 July 1976; Moss, 'Why Prior must go', *The Free Nation*, 1977.

58   Interview with CTU national official, 10 January 1978.

59   *Conservative News*, March 1979.

60   Calcraft, op.cit.

61   Scott, 'Policies for tomorrow', *The Cambridge Reformer*, October 1977; Raison, 'The State of Conservatism', *The Round Table*, 1977, p.16.

7 Mr Heath and the development of policy

> 'the most compelling reason to support the theory that
> Mr Heath believed that history came to a full stop in
> February 1974 is that so many of Mrs Thatcher's shadow
> cabinet were equally convinced that history experienced
> a short intermission between 1970 and 1974 and did not
> begin again until February 1975'.

After 1975 the Thatcher leadership experienced difficulty in establishing legitimacy with some sections of the Conservative party, notably with people identified with Mr Heath. This chapter investigates the nature and extent of the disaffection. It is argued that the lack of harmony owed something to the Diehard-Ditcher disputation, but that other factors intervened to exacerbate the difficulties and prolong the disunity. Amongst these were the disregard certain Diehards apparently held for the Constitutional doctrine of collective cabinet responsibility, and Mr Heath's personal response to his loss of the party leadership. It will be shown that despite the Thatcher-Heath imbroglio and the Diehard-Ditcher debate, there was in fact a considerable continuity in the policy choices which the party made between 1974 and 1979. This is explained in part by Mrs Thatcher's habit of combining the expression of Diehard sentiments with a determination to proceed with caution, and in part by the consensus which existed on policy issues beneath and away from the Diehard-Ditcher disputation.

Any hope or expectation that Mrs Thatcher might have had at the conclusion of the 1975 leadership election that she would automatically become the head of a united party was rudely dispelled in the course of a courtesy call she paid on the defeated leader. The precise exchanges at this meeting are disputed but the prevalence of a cordiality befitting a duel is not.[1] Mr Heath ruled out the possibility that he might serve in the new shadow cabinet, and subsequently declined to lead the Conservative campaign for a 'yes' vote in the June 1975 referendum on Europe. He did participate vigorously in the campaign but without reference to the new Conservative leader. At the 1975 annual conference of the National Union Mr Heath caused further disquiet by making derogatory remarks about the new leadership within earshot of journalists and politicians.[2] He denied however a newspaper report that he had called Mrs Thatcher and her supporters traitors.[3] In the wake of this conference Mr Heath announced his intention to remain active in national politics, and at Folkestone he declared that by discussing a wide range of fundamental questions on public platforms and in print, he would put to constructive use the freedom he now enjoyed. He hoped that this would be for the benefit of both his party and his country.[4]

What followed was a succession of reflections which distanced the former leader from the new leadership. Mr Heath argued that Conservative education policy centred too narrowly on direct grant and independent schools which were not an option for the majority of parents and children, and that the case for private enterprise was being put across too stridently. When the Conservatives broke off co-operation through the 'usual channels' with the Government in the summer of 1976, Mr Heath rejoined that such obstruction would lose the Conservatives public support.[5] In the House of Commons Mr Heath 'fully and unequivocally' expressed support for the Labour Government's incomes policy, and he withheld any public expression of confidence in his new leader until October 1976, when at the annual conference he announced that he had 'complete confidence in Margaret Thatcher and her (shadow cabinet) colleagues on the platform' who would 'not flinch in future in taking difficult decisions that are in the national interest'.[6] Even this apparent gesture of reconciliation was embedded in a speech devoted in part to self justification and coalition kite flying, and was certainly not a prescription for a return to an era of good feelings.

The 'agony' continued to unfold with Mr Heath criticising Diehard attacks on both the 'shirkers' who scrounged off social security benefits and on those Labour MPs with Marxist sympathies. 'Our party', Mr Heath affirmed, 'must not revel in the squalor of this sort of approach. We have to be positive'. Being positive also involved Mr Heath in defying the Conservative party's three line whip instructing MPs to oppose the Government's Scotland and Wales Bill. Mr Heath said that it was unthinkable that those Conservatives like himself who had long believed in the principle of devolution should be expected to vote against the second reading. What was needed was 'meaningful' devolution, and the bill went a long way to establishing it.[7] When revised provisions were introduced a year later following the demise of the first legislative effort, Mr Heath was travelling around the country promoting two of his books.[8]

Reinvigorated by his meet-the-people tour, Mr Heath turned his attention to Mrs Thatcher's statements on immigration at the commencement of 1978. Interviewed on television at the end of January,

Mrs Thatcher had made four important points: immigration was too high, people were afraid that Britain might be 'swamped' by people of a different culture, the Conservative party would hold out the prospect of an end to immigration except for compassionate cases, and there was a feeling that the big political parties were not talking enough about the issue. Mrs Thatcher elaborated on these themes at the Young Conservatives' conference in Harrogate and said that the Conservatives would honour in full legal commitments to United Kingdom passport holders in East Africa and to the immediate dependants of those who settled in Britain before 1973.[9] Mr Heath leapt into the fray. He was glad that the Conservative party was going to adhere to the commitments made during his own administration to East African passport holders and dependants, but he resented the suggestion that the large parties did not discuss immigration. In 1971 Parliament had spent nine months discussing it, and the resultant Act gave Parliament complete power to do what it liked on the subject. Mr Heath added that the suggestion from some Conservatives that there should be a ban on the male fiancés of women already settled in Britain ill became anyone who was critical of Russian flaunting of the Helsinki (human rights) Agreement. (Earlier in the week following a difficult time experienced by Mrs Thatcher during Prime Minister's questions in the House of Commons, the normally impassive Mr Heath responded to the observation by Mr Dennis Skinner that 'She's having a rough afternoon, isn't she, Ted?' with what one political correspondent described as a grin and a 'huge, meaningful wink'.)[10]

Following this sortie, Mr Heath informed Conservatives in Penistone that he would 'continue' to fight for the Conservative party though it would still need to show that it was broadly based. In October 1978 however, he re-emphasised his differences with the party leadership by alleging that official Conservative economic policies 'just don't work'. He endorsed the Government's incomes policy pay limit of 5 per cent and said that governments could not leave pay bargaining to employers and employees. Furthermore, if the Labour Prime Minister went to the country on the grounds that he wanted to prevent another wages 'free-for-all', then Mr Heath indicated that on that substantive point he would not oppose the Prime Minister. At the party conference Mr Heath warned Conservatives against gloating at the collapse of the Government's incomes policy. If it had broken down, 'we should grieve for our country'.[11] Subsequently, in the run up to the 1979 general election, Mr Heath campaigned hard for the Conservative cause, but the words 'Margaret Thatcher' passed his lips with the frequency of a partial eclipse of the sun.

Within the Parliamentary party the reactions to Mr Heath's dissent varied over time, and across the spectrum of Conservatism. In the months following the leadership election there was considerable Ditcher sympathy for Mr Heath especially against the background of the speedy disassociation by Sir Keith Joseph and Mrs Thatcher from the actions of the Heath Government. They had after all been collectively responsible for the policies of the Heath administration and chosen not to resign. As one of Mr Heath's close associates pointed out in reference to Sir Keith Joseph's discovery of 'true' Conservatism after February 1974, 'There was nothing dishonest about what he did. He just said, "I was wrong, I was wrong", and beat his chest in self-condemnation. It was rather a matter of lack of judgement to turn round and denounce what the (Heath) cabinet had done and what he himself had done as Secretary of State.' This was 'foolish' and caused great 'resentment'.[12] This denounciation did not abate with the election of Mrs Thatcher and according to Mr Douglas Hurd, associates of both the new leader and Sir Keith Joseph launched a 'crude' and 'unnecessary' assault on the record of the Heath administration.[13] These assaults clearly annoyed Ditcher MPs, and one described them as 'absolutely disgraceful and utterly foolish'.[14]

As time went by however, this sympathy began to give way to a growing resentment at Mr Heath's aloofness and dissent. One senior Conservative whip commented in February 1976, 'I feel desperately sorry for Ted, but there is a feeling in the party that he has not behaved in the right way'.[15] The whip explained that Mr Heath's aloofness was interpreted by Conservative MPs as a sign of contempt for them. A number of MPs interviewed acquiesced in this view. They believed that Mr Heath held them in contempt and emphasised that he had behaved 'disgracefully' or at least with a 'lack of grace'.[16] Other MPs were content to concede simply that the parliamentary party had grown 'tired' of Mr Heath's dissent.[17] The criticism was certainly not confined to Diehards. Speaking in October 1976 one of Mr Heath's Ditcher admirers in the House of Commons considered that his dissent had gone on 'rather too long',[18] while another cabinet colleague and Ditcher stalwart described the behaviour of his friend as 'unwise' and 'ungracious'. The latter indicated that Mr Heath had not behaved well and that he had told him so to his face. Mr Heath should have told Mrs Thatcher that he was tired and needed a rest, but that in a couple of years he would serve in the shadow cabinet if needed, as he was always willing to serve the party. However, it was pointed out that 'alas that was not in Edward's character. Instead by his demeanour he was guilty of "adultery" by intention if not in substance'.[19]

It is important to point out that some Conservative MPs would have been hostile to Mr Heath regardless of his behaviour after 1975. The memories of his leadership style and of the electoral defeat in February 1974 were fresh in the mind and there were one or two shadow ministers, for example, 'who would not forgive Mr Heath if he came crawling in front of them on his hands and knees'.[20] In this sense there is no need to examine Mr Heath's behaviour after 1975 to pinpoint what caused the resentment, since the ill feeling was ready and waiting. Nevertheless certain of Mr Heath's actions, real or perceived, and the effect of them, clearly exacerbated an abiding disaffection. There was first the feeling that Mr Heath's alienation was electorally disadvantageous for the Conservative party. This feeling came to the fore after the Conservatives failed to win the 1978 Berwick and East Lothian by-election following the disagreement at the party conference over pay policy. Mr George Gardiner, the Diehard publicist, suggested that 'the sad conclusion' from Berwick was that Mr Heath's public disagreement with the rest of the Conservative party was doing the opposition serious harm.[21] An editorial in the *Conservative Agents Journal* agreed, and from the shadow cabinet Mr Teddy Taylor had to warn Conservatives not to indulge in a witch hunt.[22] Second, there was a feeling that Mr Heath was engaged, either on his own or with the assistance of others, in an attempt to bring the leadership of Mrs Thatcher to an early conclusion. As to the first possibility one of Mr Heath's friends thought that the former Conservative leader at least retained the hope that a national coalition government might be formed, long after he had proposed the idea in October 1974.[23] This might have had ramifications for Mrs Thatcher's leadership. The second possibility also caused disquiet and there were times, in 1975 and 1976, when those around Mrs Thatcher thought in terms of a Heath camp.[24] The foundation of the Tory Reform Group (TRG) — an amalgamation of PEST (Pressure for Economic and Social Toryism), the Iain Macleod Group, and STAG (Social Tory Action Group) — caused a few flutters, particularly when it appeared on the scene in the autumn of 1975 with prominent Ditchers like Mr Peter Walker, Mr Nicholas Scott and Lord Carr amongst its ranks. Mr John Nott, one of Mrs Thatcher's Diehard shadow ministers, complained vaguely from Cornwall of 'a minor irritation' in the form of a small anti-Thatcher group 'which sometimes seems to give needless support to our opponents in the country'.[25] If this was an attack on associates of the TRG it was quickly rebutted. Mr Peter Walker told a group meeting that he was 'astounded, amused, amazed and annoyed' by suggestions that the TRG was anti-Thatcher.[26] A Conservative whip evidently agreed for he confirmed in February 1976 that Mr Walker and Mr Scott were 'behaving themselves perfectly' whatever their convictions about the Ditcher cause.[27] In general there appears to have been little substance to the suggestion of a Ditcher conspiracy. One Ditcher shadow minister dismissed by Mrs Thatcher on her elevation to the leadership said that there had been little contact between the supposed leading Ditcher conspirators. He (the dismissed Ditcher) had hoped that Mr Walker, Mr Scott, Lord Carr, Mr Lane and Mr Heath would keep in touch 'and at least have a drink now and then', but this had not happened and Mr Heath had withdrawn completely while he was so hurt.[28]

A third irritation was Mr Heath's tendency to legitimise his opposition to the official Conservative line on the grounds of strongly held personal conviction. This was the justification for his deviation from the party line on devolution (see above p.104) and caused Mr Biggs-Davison, a Suez rebel when Mr Heath was Chief Whip, to suggest wryly that at long last the formidable gamekeeper had turned poacher. The Diehard, Sir Frederic Bennett, was less subtle and expressed the opinion that those who served under Mr Heath could recall that he 'only encouraged, indeed permitted, others similarly to uphold their convictions so long as they happened to coincide with his own'. The same point was made by Mr Jock Bruce-Gardyne who reflected on Mr Heath's justification for dissent from party pay policy on the grounds that it 'had never been the case' that policy was handed down from on high and accepted by everyone. Mr Bruce-Gardyne (a Diehard crusader) did not recall that this had been Mr Heath's own attitude to those Conservatives who disputed wage controls in 1972.[29]

What did the picture look like from Mr Heath's perspective? One of Mrs Thatcher's shadow ministers who voted for Mr Heath in 1975 explained that he and other Conservatives did not defend the actions of the Heath administration after 1975 because they were frightened of becoming involved 'in the dispute over Mr Heath'. As a result, in the House of Commons many of the Labour criticisms of the Heath Government went by default.[30] Mr Heath had therefore to stomach not only (what Mr Hurd had called) the crude and unnecessary attacks on his own Government from his own side, but a reluctance by his colleagues to sustain him from the attacks of the Labour opposition. This set of circumstances did not exactly please him. He wrote that if the Conservative party did not defend its own record in Government, nobody else would: 'It is one thing to admit past mistakes; that is sensible. It's quite another for Conservatives to go round the country wearing sack-cloth and ashes, apologising for mistakes which are so blatantly of Labour's own making'.[31]

Second, from the moment Mr Heath was defeated in the leadership election he was extremely worried that all the things he had stood for as leader might be pushed away, and that the Conservative party would become an entirely different creature.[32] One of his colleagues (dismissed by Mrs Thatcher) explained that this was why Mr Heath had not entered the shadow cabinet in 1975, and why it was so inappropriate to remind Mr Heath of the example of Sir Alec Douglas Home in loyally serving the new Conservative leader in 1965:[33] Sir Alec had not been opposed to the new leader's policies.[34] What made matters more delicate was that Mrs Thatcher's determination not to make detailed policy commitments meant that it was less than easy to judge just where the Conservative party stood on important issues. As Mr Geoffrey Rippon pointed out in Mr Heath's defence in June 1976, it was difficult to establish party unity while policy was still in the air.[35]

The continuity of policy

Given the anxieties expressed by Mr Heath it is important to establish just how far Conservative policies changed with the elevation of Mrs Thatcher. In chapter 2 we saw the hopes and expectations articulated by Diehards for a radical departure in Conservative politics. In chapter 5 it was shown that Conservative economic policy took on a liberal and Diehard flavour in that it emphasised the importance of the market, monetarism, public spending cuts and cash limits. This was a significant development but Mrs Thatcher was careful not to decisively reject incomes policy as a future possibility. In chapter 6 we saw that despite Diehard grumblings Conservative employment law policy showed a substantial amount of continuity between 1974 and 1979. In other areas of dispute between Diehards and Ditchers, the Conservatives showed a similar tendency to declaim with the roar of a lion and to move with less certainty. Industrial policy was a case in point. In the wake of declarations by Sir Keith Joseph and Mrs Thatcher about the need to rely upon the genius of the market economy and to resist the funding of inefficient industry (see above, chapters 2 and 5), Conservative policy did show a Diehard flavour, but it was littered with escape routes to enough interventionism to keep most Ditchers acquiescent.

With regard to industrial subsidies the Conservatives stated that 'In general, we believe that when firms cannot get out of their difficulties themselves the situation is not improved if everyone believes that a tax-financed solution is ready to hand'. This statement had certain ramifications for the future of Labour created interventionist mechanisms. In 1976, for example, Conservatives pledged to abolish the National Enterprise Board (NEB) and retain only an administrative mechanism for selling off those NEB shareholdings which could be sold or for administering those which could not. Such a body would have no innovating powers of its own. This declaration was modified somewhat by 1979 when the NEB was no longer to be abolished but was to have its powers restricted. The Conservatives also pledged to amend the 1975 Industry Act with its disclosure provisions and planning agreements. This again constituted a modification from the 1976 intention to repeal the Act altogether. The powers of the Scottish and Welsh Development

Agencies to buy into profitable companies were to be removed, and with regard to nationalisation, as much as possible of the interests of British Shipbuilders and British Aerospace (taken into public ownership after 1974) were to be sold off to the private sector.[36]

These declarations of withdrawal from intervention were however matched with a clear statement that 'we . . . recognise too that there will be some exceptional cases where help (through subsidies) may be justified in the national interest'. Such help would be both 'temporary and tapered', but Sir Geoffrey Howe stressed that there would be no 'sharp or sudden changes' in subsidies and that existing commitments would be honoured.[37] Furthermore, as far as the giant lame duck of British Leyland was concerned, the Conservatives pledged to continue to subsidise it. Mr Prior put the matter squarely: 'We want BL to succeed. We back Michael Edwardes and his managers, and admire the efforts he and his team have been making to pull the firm round . . . We have always said and say again, that BL needs to be given a proper chance'. Mrs Thatcher was no less forthright. She pointed out that she believed that British taxpayers were prepared to put their hands in their pockets to help BL, 'if BL show that they are prepared to help themselves. This is the attitude which we would take in government.'[38] Conservative industrial policy was therefore Diehard in tone but careful not to proscribe interventionism in 'the national interest'. Legislative axes were waved in the direction of post-1974 Labour Government innovations, but there was not a whisper in a Conservative policy statement to suggest that Mr Heath's interventionist 1972 Industry Act would be repealed.

What consequences did Diehard rhetoric about the reinstitution of bourgeois values and the need to withdraw the boundaries of the state have for Conservative social policy? In two areas of social policy and administration, housing and penal policy, it would not be surprising to find continuity between the Heath and Thatcher eras since the consensus between Diehards and Ditchers about the importance of property and the rule of law spirited them along the same prescriptive path. Indeed, in the field of housing, the promotion of what was called a property owning democracy continued as if there had been no leadership election at all. Both leaderships after 1974 said they would give priority to granting council tenants the statutory right to buy their homes after three years occupancy, and to extending assistance to first time buyers.[39] Penal policy manifested the same incremental approach, notwithstanding an energetic (and unsuccessful) campaign conducted from within the shadow cabinet by the Diehard Mr Teddy Taylor to commit the Conservative party to a referendum on capital punishment. If there was a slight change under Mrs Thatcher it lay in greater emphasis being given to the use of prisons rather than community homes for dealing with young offenders. In general however, the strategy laid down under Mr Heath was zealously pursued. In 1974 the Conservatives had dwelt on the need to tackle the growth in crime committed by young persons. They noted that the courts should be able to deal more effectively with such offenders, and needed a wider range of institutions to send them to. Under Mrs Thatcher, the Conservative party developed these ideas. A pledge was made to amend the Children and Young Persons Act of 1969 to give magistrates the power to make residential and secure care orders on young offenders. The Criminal Justice Act of 1961 was also to be amended to allow courts to impose prison sentences of up to three years on 17-21 year old offenders. In addition, the use of attendance centres was to be expanded, and in some detention centres the regime was to be toughened – on an experimental basis – to institute what Mr William Whitelaw called a 'short, sharp, shock' to violent young 'thugs'.[40]

In other areas of social policy, consensus between Diehards and Ditchers did not intervene to cause some convergence of policy views, yet even here there was a marked continuity in policy between the Heath and Thatcher leaderships. Diehards had launched fierce attacks on the National Health Service, scroungers and illiteracy (see chapter 2) yet in terms of specific policy commitments the Diehard leadership stood broadly where Mr Heath had stood after 1974. For all the Diehard assaults on the debilitating effects of the Welfare State, for example, policy for the National Health Service continued on much the same lines set out in 1974. There was certainly no firm indication given under Mrs Thatcher that resources available to the health service would be cut and Sir Geoffrey Howe went out of his way to emphasise that they would not be. The Conservatives pledged that pay beds would be allowed where there was a demand for them, and that there would be an end to Labour's supposed vendetta against the private health sector. The possibility of raising prescription charges was also countenanced. Each of these ideas constituted a restatement of policies made in 1974. The only substantial difference appears to have been that whereas the Heath leadership was in favour of a period of stability based upon the 1973 Joseph-inspired reorganisation of the health service, under Mrs Thatcher the Conservatives planned to 'simplify and decentralise the service and cut back bureaucracy'. No doubt this was a concession to Sir Keith Joseph's desire to wipe his own slate clean following his conversion to 'true' Conservatism in 1974.[41] There was little change in social security policy either. The 1974 commitment to the tax credit scheme was restated, and the only development was that the Conservatives pledged to act 'more vigorously' against fraud and abuse. This involved an increase in the number of 'fraud drives' and of special social security investigators. However, it is important to note that the Conservatives considered that the lack of incentive to work was much more damaging to public morale and more harmful to the genuine poor. The problem of 'scrounging' was therefore certainly not seen to be the be-all and end-all of equitable policy.[42] The assault on illiteracy had little effect on education policy. Under Mrs Thatcher, the Conservatives pledged themselves to raising general levels of competence and to this end they promised national standards in reading, writing and arithmetic enforced by a strengthened inspectorate. The repeal of legislation compelling local authorities to reorganise along comprehensive lines was also envisaged and this was to be accompanied by the restoration of direct grant schools 'democratised' by an assisted places scheme to facilitate entry to the children of less wealthy parents. The Conservatives also promised a parents' charter which would place a clear duty on government and local authorities to take account of the wishes of parents when allocating children to schools. Every one of these proposals had been envisaged by the Conservatives when they fought the October 1974 election under Mr Heath.[43] The last area of continuity in social policy was immigration. All the populist huffing and puffing which surrounded Mr Keith Speed's review of immigration policy in 1978 made little impression on official Conservative policy. It remained founded upon four fundamental principles which had been outlined in 1974. These were first, that better community relations depended upon strictly limited immigration and second, that all legally settled British citizens were equal before the law whatever their colour or creed. Third, there was recognition that the party had to continue to honour legal commitments made to United Kingdom passport holders in East Africa and to the immediate dependants of all those who settled in Britain as of right before 1973. Fourth, the Conservatives upheld their promise made in 1974 that there was no question of compulsory repatriation.[44] Some of these measures (ending the concession to husbands and male fiances) were designed to safeguard against the abuse of the system about which the Conservatives had expressed concern in 1974, and some were bipartisan (quotas and firm action against illegal immigrants and overstayers) at least in the sense that they had been suggested by the all party select committee on race relations in 1978. In any event, as Mr Reginald Maudling pointed out, the new Conservative proposals would only reduce the flow of immigrants by about 5,000 a year. As this amounted to one less immigrant for every 11,000 people already living in Britain, and as the increase in the coloured population would occur through their 'natural procreation' the Conservative proposals under Mrs Thatcher hardly represented the difference 'between being swamped and remaining on dry land'.[45]

In areas unaffected by Diehard-Ditcher disputes, Conservative policy again developed along lines outlined by Mr Heath. This is well illustrated by reference to Conservative attitudes towards external affairs and decentralisation. Mr Heath had conceived of Britain's relationship with the world as rooted in three important activities: a firm commitment towards the NATO alliance in the light of the growth of the Soviet armed forces, vigorous participation within the European Economic Community, and the development of Britain's relationship with China. Each of these policies was endorsed and followed by the Conservative party under Mrs Thatcher. When, for example, Mr Callaghan came close to hinting in 1976 that the British military presence in Germany was contingent upon reciprocal credit from the friends and allies of Britain, Sir Ian Gilmour, the Ditcher shadow defence spokesman inveighed against the Prime Minister's 'act of craven folly' and 'wanton abrogation of his prime responsibility for our security'. It was as if 'the deranged captain of a sinking ship had ordered the lifeboats to be jettisoned rather than the ballast'. Similar opprobrium was directed towards Labour plans for defence cuts. According to Sir Ian these amounted to 'completely irresponsible rubbish' and Mrs Thatcher summed up the response of the Labour Government to the growing military peril of the West as 'dedicated negligence'. In a speech which won her international notice in January 1976, Mrs Thatcher stressed that the first duty of any government was to safeguard its people against external aggression, and that Britain urgently needed to strengthen her defences.[46]

On the question of Britain and Europe, while Mrs Thatcher cannot be said to have duplicated Mr Heath's European zeal, she made it clear that under her direction the Conservative party would continue to strive to be the European party in Britain, and that the Conservatives wanted to co-operate 'whole-heartedly' with their partners in the EEC venture. The parameters set by the idea of wholehearted co-operation were clearly defined. Europe, Mrs Thatcher explained, should continue to be a partnership of nation states 'each retaining the right to protect its vital interests, but developing more effectively than at present the habit of working together'. This denial of the prospect of federalism, at least for the immediate future, enabled even European sceptics like Mr John Biffen and Mr Teddy Taylor to reconcile themselves to the EEC. As Mr Biffen pointed out, a 'Europe des Patries' was no longer a fading Gaullist dream, but 'the inexorable and unavoidable goal of European co-operation'.[47] Within this wide parameter the Conservatives were able to display a firm commitment to Europe, and this displayed itself in several ways. First, although the Conservatives opposed the idea of a referendum on EEC membership, once it was clear that the referendum would take place, the party launched an enthusiastic campaign for an endorsement of membership. Mrs Thatcher explained her own low profile in this campaign not in terms of lack of conviction about Europe, but as a (possibly mistaken) reaction to what she called the embarrassing problem of having to shore up an unenthusiastic and divided Government. Second, the Conservatives urged the speedy passage of the European Assemblies Bill to facilitate the holding of direct elections to the European Parliament. To this end they even took the unusual step of supporting a Government guillotine motion in January 1978. (Most Conservatives did however oppose the provision in the Bill for elections based on a regional list system. This might have been quicker to set up than the first-past-the-post arrangement with its attendant appeals for constituency boundaries.) Third, the Conservatives argued that the best way to voice criticisms of the EEC was not to adopt the Labour Government's position of slithering 'unhappily between bluster and back-sliding' but first to obtain the position of a trusted and committed partner. Within this context the Conservatives said they would seek to make changes in three important aspects of community life. The first was the common Agricultural Policy. According to Mr Biffen this was 'collapsing under the weight of its own surpluses', and even a dedicated Conservative European like Mr Christopher Tugenhat (who was appointed to the European Commission in 1977) admitted that it needed to be reformed.[48] The 1979 Conservative Manifesto proposed the devaluation of the Green Pound 'within the normal lifetime of a Parliament to a point which would enable our producers to compete on level terms with those in the rest of the Community'. The Conservatives also thought that national payments into the community budget should be more closely related to ability to pay, and last, they railed against excessive community bureaucracy. As Mrs Thatcher noted in Brussels, the idea of European unity was a grand concept but 'the cause of unity is surely not advanced by hundreds of petty internal regulations, such as the content of ice cream or the activities of doorstep salesmen'. Overall the official Conservative policy maintained the commitment to Europe to the satisfaction of Conservative Europeans but without alienating the increasing number in the party who, according to one shadow minister, though that 'a kind of Gaullist, obstinate, national response was the best way of approaching the problem'.[49]

The third strand of Mr Heath's foreign policy, the rapprochement with China, was also endorsed by Mrs Thatcher. She emulated her predecessor by paying a visit to the Peoples Republic, traced his steps along the Great Wall and made suitable attempts to handle chopsticks. Mrs Thatcher stressed that although China was hardly a member of the golden club of democracies and although Britain was as philosophically estranged from her as she was from the Soviet Union, 'we can recognise that China is not an expansionist power like Russia, and she does not pose a threat to us. Our present friendship with China can only have beneficial consequences both for our people, and hers'.[50] Evidently Mr Heath's sorties to the Chinese mainland were no temporary aberration.

One subject which occupied a large amount of time and energy after 1974 was decentralisation, particularly in the way it affected the government of Northern Ireland and Scotland. While there is little doubt that the bipartisan stance on Northern Ireland displayed by the Conservative party under Mr Heath was continued under Mrs Thatcher, the continuity in Scottish policy is more difficult to establish. The creation and subsequent collapse, in May 1974, of a power sharing executive in Northern Ireland had important consequences for British politics. In the first place it marked the fragmentation of the Ulster Unionist Party in Northern Ireland and the severing of Unionist ties with the Conservative party in Britain. In terms of practical politics this meant that after February 1974 Unionist MPs did not take the Conservative whip at Westminster, and that Conservative party managers were continually in doubt about Unionist voting intentions.[51] Second, the collapse of the executive led to the reinstitution of direct rule. This involved the use of executive powers by ministers from the Northern Ireland Office, and meant that Northern Ireland was therefore deprived of a continuing Unionist demand — a devolved Parliament and Government.

Following the collapse of the power sharing executive the Labour Government announced the setting up of a constitutional convention to give Northern Irish representatives the opportunity to recommend to Westminster an agreed constitutional formula. A majority report was voted through the convention by Unionists opposed to power sharing. It proposed the restoration of a devolved Parliament with a government responsible to it which consisted of only those loyal to the political integrity of Northern Ireland. The Labour Government concluded that these recommendations would not win sufficiently widespread acceptance throughout the province to facilitate stable and effective government.[52] In these circumstances the Conservative party might have been tempted to abandon bipartisanhip and to have held out to the Ulster Unionists the prospect of an immediate return to a devolved assembly for Northern Ireland. The party did after all have what Mrs Thatcher called 'historic links' with the Ulster Unionists, and the manoeuvre could have been legitimised by being represented as 'what Lord Randolph Churchill or Andrew Bonar Law would have done'. In the event the Conservatives did no such thing. Mr Neave acquiesced in the Labour Government's rejection of the majority convention report and satisfied himself thereafter with the vague commitment to encourage talks amongst the political parties in Northern Ireland, to pave the way for a devolved form of government which for the present remained 'unattainable'. Lord Randolph Churchill was left in the cupboard.[53]

As a way of compensation to the Ulster Unionists Mr Neave and Mrs Thatcher lost no opportunity to reaffirm their commitment to the Union, to press for extra seats for Northern Ireland at Westminster, and to talk about Conservative plans to restore the upper tier of local government which had been removed from democratic control in October 1973. Each of these activities was bipartisan (the Labour party accepted extra Northern Irish representation from 1977), though Mr Neave's assault on the Government's security policy in Northern Ireland was not. Mr Neave was particularly critical of the 'cease-fire' negotiated through Provisional Sinn Fein with the IRA in February 1975, and with the direction of SAS operations in South Armagh in 1976. Overall however, Mr Neave concluded that bipartisanship on most issues had stood up well. Mr Heath's view was not repudiated.[54]

Whether or not Mr Heath's views disavowed on the question of devolution for Scotland is more problematical. There is certainly no doubt that following her early endorsement, in May 1975, of the Conservative party's commitment to a directly elected assembly, Mrs Thatcher embarked upon a careful retreat. The endorsement of an elected assembly was restated by Mr William Whitelaw in Perth in May 1976. However, while the Labour Government was preparing a form of decentralisation based on the majority report of the Kilbrandon Commission and involving an assembly with an attendant executive, Mr Whitelaw stressed that the shadow cabinet had less ambitious proposals. They envisaged that their assembly would be an additional chamber of the Westminster Parliament involved in putting new legislation and government in Scotland to scrutiny. No new executive was to be created. These proposals were summed up by Mr John Biffen as involving 'an Assembly in Edinburgh whose modest powers could not conceivably rival or challenge the authority of Westminster', and were repeated in *The Right Approach*.[55] Up to this time some pro-devolutionists were still to be heard expressing their 'absolute delight' at the firmness of the party's commitment to an assembly. The suspicion that they were merely whistling in the dark to keep up their spirits was confirmed in December 1976 when Mrs Thatcher announced that her party would oppose the second reading of the Scotland and Wales Bill with a three line whip. This was too much for Mr Buchanan-Smith, the pro-devolutionist shadow Scottish Secretary and he resigned (along with the front bench spokesman Mr Malcolm Rifkind) and was replaced by Mr Teddy Taylor. Mr Taylor proceeded to announce that while the Conservatives would oppose the Scotland and Wales Bill 'we will reaffirm absolutely and without hesitation the party's support for a directly elected assembly in Scotland'.

To those who had watched Mr Taylor's spirited and good natured attack on Scottish assemblies at successive party conferences it was obvious that either Mr Taylor had undergone a sudden conversion or that Conservative policy was about to move on. There was no sudden conversion, and within a few weeks of Mr Taylor's appointment the shadow cabinet had announced its proposal of an all party convention on decentralisation, entered into 'without any pre-conditions . . . without any pre-commitment to a particular policy'.[56] From this point the Conservatives were committed to very little besides talking. When the Scotland Bill was introduced in November 1977 (following the demise of the Scotland and Wales Bill) the Conservatives again opposed the measure and called for a constitutional convention to spend six months discussing the problem. In the second reading debate Mr Taylor emphasised that the Conservatives were opposed to the specific legislation and not to the principle of devolution. Throughout the passage of the legislation Conservatives joined with Labour dissidents in amending the Bill. Concurrently, in February 1978, Mr Pym expanded on the options a constitutional convention might consider. These included the establishment of a new select committee for Scottish MPs, a non-legislative assembly with powers of scrutiny, home rule all-round, and executive or legislative devolution for Scotland alone.[57] Official policy therefore did not rule out, after talks, the possibility of a Scottish assembly with its own cabinet, but 'that would have to be on the basis of an explicit acceptance by the House of Commons *and the people of England* of the anomolies thus created'. The Scotland Act did not meet these conditions, not least because it provided for a referendum in Scotland but not in England, and the shadow cabinet pressed for a 'no' vote in the referendum of March 1979. Mrs Thatcher again emphasised that this did not mean that devolution would be buried as an issue and, following the inconclusive referendum result and the fall of the Government, the 1979 manifesto announced 'We are committed to discussions about the future government of Scotland'.[58]

To what extent can this cautious retreat be considered a significant departure from the Heath years? Certainly after February 1975 Mr Heath drew a picture of himself as one who had nurtured a 'long and deeply-held' belief that within the United Kingdom Scotland should achieve 'full and effective' devolution. Given such commitment then, the Thatcher shuffle was significant. However, there is a case for suggesting that like most politicians in the 1960s and 1970s Mr Heath blew hot and cold on the question of Scottish devolution. Of course, as he frequently reminded people, he had been early on the scene and committed the Conservative party to the creation of a directly elected assembly in Perth in May 1968. Nevertheless there was no commitment to a directly elected assembly in the Conservative party manifesto of October 1974. Furthermore large sections of the Conservative party showed little enthusiasm for Scottish devolution after 1968, and did not need much prompting from Mrs Thatcher or Mr Pym, to alter their policy. Looked at from this perspective the change was hardly momentous.[59]

Across the broad range of policies therefore, continuity was the order of the day. If Mr Heath was worried in 1975 that the Conservative party would overthrow everything he had stood for, then it should have become increasingly apparent, notwithstanding Diehard speech-making, that caution and incrementalism were the hallmark of the Thatcher leadership. It was this caution which went a good way to reconciling most of the Ditchers, including Mr Prior and Sir Ian Gilmour to Mrs Thatcher's leadership. Mr Maudling said in 1975 that he would be 'delighted' to serve under Mrs Thatcher and another Ditcher, for example, who held broadly similar views to Mr Heath found no difficulty in serving as a front bench spokesman. He had carefully considered his position after Mr Heath's defeat and identified four policies which would prevent him from serving under the new leader: these were the overthrow of the commitment to Europe, the end of bi-partisanship over Ulster, a repeal of the 1972 Industry Act and a categoric statement ruling out the possibility of a statutory incomes policy.[60] None of these policies ever materialised, and this Ditcher served on the front bench without interruption after February 1975, and with some distinction.

Of course what caused concern to Ditchers, whether or not they served (or were invited to serve) was the Diehard *tone* of the Thatcher leadership. The articulation of Diehard opinions (reported in chapter 2) left a string of Ditchers concerned about the image this was creating for the Conservative party. Mr Peter Walker warned that Labour would not be won over by a recitation of extracts from the works of Milton Friedman, Mr Nicholas Scott deprecated the 'siren voices calling for a distinctive road', and Mr Reginald Maudling, conscious that there was a growing feeling that the party might be 'difficult, abrasive and divisive' in government, counselled Conservatives against adopting policies more appropriate to nineteenth century liberalism. Even Lord Hailsham warned against excessive concentration on Diehard thought.[61] And these expressions of concern were not made without good cause. Mrs Thatcher's particular skill lay in flying a Diehard kite and then carrying on, leaving policy unchanged or merely adjusted at the margin. Immigration was a case in point. We have seen that there was virtually no change in policy in this area. However, by using a word like 'swamped' (twice) on television, and by talking about 'a clear end to immigration', the Conservative leader created the impression that policy had changed. Mr William Whitelaw then stepped in to say to blacks, browns and Conservative social scientists that he preferred to use the phrase 'an end to immigration as we know it', and that 'I do not believe anybody can say that nobody can ever come in, and I do not think she meant that'.[62] By then, of course, Mrs Thatcher's kite flying had already served its purpose and the original impression was not dispelled. There were those who maintained that Mrs Thatcher had merely made a slip of the tongue, or was unbriefed but giving a straight answer to a straight question. We shall see, in chapter 8, that this was to do Mrs Thatcher a serious injustice.

In any event Mr Heath was not alone in being disquieted by the Diehard flavour of Conservative politics after 1975. We have seen that he distanced himself further from the new leadership than any of his colleagues and that to some extent he had particular reasons for doing so. In the wake of Conservative attacks upon his own person and administration, and in some cases from those who had shared collective cabinet responsibility with him, Mr Heath could reasonably conclude, and he did, that the Conservative gunfire was impressive, but that the cannons were pointed in the wrong direction. Diehards and some Ditchers suggested that there was one last reason for Mr Heath's alienation, and that this had more to do with psychology than with political thought. According to one shadow minister, after 1975 Mr Heath became 'a poor obsessed man who is desperate to have it go down in history that the 1970-74 Government was a golden age'. As a result in the House of Commons there was a mixture of 'sorrow, anger and contempt' for him, and for the majority of MPs it was a question of 'a certain amount of sorrow'.[63] The argument that for Mr Edward Heath history stopped in 1974 has a number of attractions. In his response to Mrs Thatcher's comments on immigration, for example, Mr Heath seemed to take most displeasure from the suggestion that people felt that the big political parties had not been talking about the issue. His rejoinder that Parliament had spent nine months talking about immigration in 1971 was clearly the remark of a man bent on self-justification. In addition Mr Heath seemed to spend a lot of his time after 1975 staging a re-run of the arguments of the February of 1974 general election about 'who governs?' This was particularly true of Mr Heath's speeches in the 1979 general election campaign. Perhaps, however, the most compelling reason to support the theory that Mr Heath believed that history came to a full stop in February 1974 is that so many of Mrs Thatcher's shadow cabinet were equally convinced that history experienced a short intermission between 1970 and 1974 and did not begin again until February 1975: castigas turpia, cum sis inter Socraticos notissma Fossa cinaedos?[64]

Notes

1   Money, *Margaret Thatcher: First Lady of the House*, 1975, p.99; interview with Heath minister, 6 April 1977.

2   Interview with Conservative whip, 26 February 1976.

3   Aitken, '"Traitor" remark denied', *The Guardian*, 9 October 1975.

4   Heath, Folkestone, quoted in *The Times*, 17 November 1975.

5   Heath, quoted in *The Daily Telegraph*, 15 December 1975; Heath, quoted in *The Sunday Times*, 18 January 1976; Heath, quoted in *The Daily Telegraph*, 5 July 1976.

6   *Hansard*, 7 July 1976, col.1412; Heath, *CCVR*, 1976, p.64.

7   Clark, 'Mr Heath criticizes "negative attitudes"', *The Times*, 18 November 1976; Heath, quoted in *The Daily Telegraph*, 7 December 1976.

8   *The Sunday Telegraph*, 11 December 1977.

9   Thatcher, quoted in *The Guardian*, 31 January 1978; Thatcher, quoted in *The Times*, 13 February 1978.

10   Hoggart, 'Heath spurns the Thatcher line on immigration', *The Guardian*, 14 February 1978.

11   Heath, quoted in *The Guardian*, 9 October 1978; Heath on television, quoted in *The Daily Mail*, 12 October 1978; Heath, *CCVR*, 1978, quoted in *The Times*, 12 October 1978.

12   Interview with Conservative MP, 27 October 1976.

13   Hurd, 'Heath's Downing Street years', *The Illustrated London News*, February 1976, p.33.

14   Interview with Conservative MP, 8 June 1976.

15   Interview with Conservative whip, 26 February 1976.

16   Interview with Conservative MP, 26 February 1976; ibid., 20 January 1978.

17   Ibid., 20 October 1976.

18   Ibid., 27 October 1976.

19   Interview with Heath minister, 6 April 1977.

20   Interview with Conservative MP, 20 October 1976.

21   Gardiner MP, quoted in *The Times*, 28 October 1978.

22   Short, editorial, *Conservative Agents Journal*, no.650, November 1978; Taylor MP, quoted in *The Sunday Times*, 29 October 1978.

23   Interview with Conservative MP, 27 October 1976.

24   Interview with member of Thatcher's private office, 17 November 1976; interview with Heath minister, 8 June 1976.

25   Nott MP, quoted in *The Observer*, 5 October 1975.

26   Walker, quoted in *The Guardian*, 10 October 1975.

27   Interview with Conservative whip, 26 February 1976.

28   Interview with dismissed shadow minister, 6 April 1977.

29   Biggs-Davison MP, quoted in *The Times*, 8 December 1976;

Bennett MP, quoted in *The Times*, 11 December 1976; Bruce-Gardyne, 'Let's talk to Ted', *The Spectator*, 28 October 1978.

30   Interview with Conservative MP, 20 January 1978.

31   Heath, 'Why is it always everyone's fault but Harold's?', *The Sunday Express*, 29 February 1976.

32   Interview with Conservative MP, 27 October 1976.

33   'If Mr Heath were to give one-tenth of the loyalty and support to Mrs Thatcher that Sir Alec gave to him, he could think of himself as a truly honourable man.' Brotherton MP, *The Times*, 17 November 1975.

34   Interview with Conservative MP, 8 June 1976.

35   Rippon, quoted in *The Times*, 14 June 1976.

36   *The Right Approach to the Economy*, 1977, p.46; *The Right Approach*, 1976, p.32; *The Conservative Manifesto*, 1979, p.15; CRD *Daily Notes*, 26 April 1979; *The Right Approach*, 1976, p.32.

37   *The Right Approach to the Economy*, 1977, p.46; *The Conservative Manifesto*, 1979, pp 14-15; Howe, Oxted, 11 April 1979, quoted in CRD, *Daily Notes*, 18 April 1979, pp 56-7.

38   Prior, Chiswick, 25 April 1979, quoted in CRD, *Daily Notes*, 28 April 1979, p.12; Thatcher, CCO *News Service*, GE 599/79, 19 April 1979.

39   *Putting Britain First*, 1974, pp 16-17; *The Right Approach*, 1976, pp 51-2; *The Conservative Manifesto*, 1979, p.23.

40   *Putting Britain First*, 1974, p.28; CRD, *Daily Notes*, 26 April 1979; *The Conservative Manifesto*, 1979, pp 19-20.

41   Howe, op.cit., pp 53-7; *The Conservative Manifesto*, 1979, p.26; *The Right Approach*, 1976, p.60; *Putting Britain First*, 1974, p.20.

42   *The Conservative Manifesto*, 1979, p.27; *Putting Britain First*, 1974, p.19; *The Right Approach*, 1976, p.58.

43   *The Conservative Manifesto*, 1979, pp 25-6; *Putting Britain First*, 1974, pp 22-3.

44   Ibid., p.26; *The Conservative Manifesto*, 1979, p.20; Thatcher to Young Conservatives, Harrogate, quoted in *The Times*, 13 February 1978.

45   Maudling, 'Why the immigration argument should stop now', *The Times*, 13 April 1978.

46   Gilmour, quoted in CRD, *The Campaign Guide*, 1977, pp 600, 601; Thatcher, Birmingham, 19 April 1979, CRD, *Daily Notes*, pp 142-3; Thatcher, Kensington, quoted in CRD, *The Campaign Guide*, 1977, p.602.

47   Thatcher, *Europe As I See It*, 1977, p.6; Thatcher, *Europa*, January 1977, quoted in *The Campaign Guide*, 1977, p.610; Biffen, *Political Office or Political Power?*, 1977, p.20.

48   Thatcher interviewed by Shrimsley, *The Daily Mail*, 12 June 1975; Hurd, Norwich, 20 March 1976, quoted in *The Campaign Guide*, 1977,

p.610; *The Conservative Manifesto*, 1979, p.30; Biffen, quoted in *The Daily Telegraph*, 27 March 1979; Tugenhat, *Conservatives in Europe*, 1979.

49   *The Conservative Manifesto*, 1979, pp 17, 30; Thatcher, *The Sinews of Foreign Policy*, 1978, p.6; interview with shadow minister, 15 February 1978.

50   Thatcher, *The Sinews of Foreign Policy*, 1978, p.3.

51   Interview with Conservative whip, 26 February 1976.

52   Rees, *Hansard*, 12 January 1976, col.54.

53   *The Right Approach*, 1976, pp 46-7; Neave, 'Bridging the gap', *The Guardian*, 3 May 1978.

54   Thatcher to Ulster Unionist Council, Belfast, CCO *News Service*, 819/78, 19 June 1978; Neave, *Hansard*, 25 March 1976, col.655; Neave, 'Bridging the gap', *The Guardian*, 3 May 1978.

55   Whitelaw, Perth, quoted in *The Campaign Guide*, 1977, p.521; Biffen, *A Nation in Doubt*, 1976, p.49; *The Right Approach*, 1976, p.49.

56   Interview with Scottish Conservative MP, 20 October 1976; Taylor, quoted in *The Times*, 9 December 1976; Pym, 19 February 1977, quoted in *The Campaign Guide*, 1977, p.521.

57   Taylor, *Hansard*, 14 November 1977, col.185; Pym, quoted in *The Guardian*, 7 February 1978.

58   Pym, quoted in *The Times*, 13 May 1978; Thatcher, quoted in *The Guardian*, 28 February 1979; *The Conservative Manifesto*, 1979, p.21.

59   Heath, Glasgow, 6 December 1976, quoted in *The Daily Telegraph*, 7 December 1976; Jordan, 'The committee stage of the Scotland and Wales Bill (1976-77)', *The Waverley Paper 1*, occasional papers, p.8.

60.   Interview with front bench spokesman, 27 October 1976.

61   Scott, 'Policies for tomorrow', *The Cambridge Reformer*, October 1977; Maudling, open letter to constituents, *The Times*, 25 November 1977; Maudling, open letter to constituents, *The Times*, 1 February 1978; Hailsham, quoted in Whiteman, 'Hailsham advice to Tories', *The Daily Telegraph*, 30 March 1977.

62   Whitelaw, quoted in *The Times*, 1 February 1978.

63   Interview with shadow minister, 15 February 1978.

64   'And do you rebuke Foul practices, when you are yourself the most notorious delving-ground among Socratic reprobates?' Juvenal *Satire II*.

8 An assessment

'in the light of his unusual self effacement and his demonstrable compassion, it might have been agreeable to discover that his conversion to "true" Conservatism in 1974 left him peerless amongst Conservatives and the recipient of universal felicitation. Coming as it did, however, in the wake of twenty years' acquiescence in and construction of something other than "true" Conservatism, it is hardly surprising to find that this was not the case'.

By the afternoon of 4 May 1979 Mrs Thatcher was ensconced in 10 Downing Street as Britain's first woman Prime Minister. It had been a quiet and serious campaign. No doubt this had something to do with the assassination of Mr Airey Neave outside the House of Commons on 30 March. The solemnity also owed something to the memories of the industrial action the previous winter. The Conservatives appealed to the electorate on the basis of a general and rather vague Diehard programme, and through the good offices of Saatchi and Saatchi laid particular emphasis on the need for (unspecified) cuts in direct taxation. The Conservative party were returned with a majority of 70 over Labour, and with an overall majority of 43 (Conservative 339, Labour 269, Liberal 11, SNP 2, PC 2, Others 12).

To all those Conservative activists who had worked hard during the campaign, the sky was never more perfectly blue, a difficult period of opposition had ended, and attention was turned to the far more pleasurable tasks of organising victory balls and speculation on the character of the new Conservative Government. Since the student of politics does not embark upon inquiry with the particular purpose of arriving at a happy ending, something more than a testimony to the hurrahs of the Conservative faithful is required. First, some concluding observations about the principal characters. To have political ambition thwarted affects politicians in different ways. When, for example, Lord Curzon was deprived of the premiership in 1923 he at least had his rich wife Grace to comfort him, and as Balfour observed 'He might have lost the hope of Glory, but he still possesses the means of Grace'.

Mr Heath was not so fortunate and, as we saw in chapter 7, not even his friends maintained that he responded well to adversity. There was some consolation for Mr Heath in the fact that at a time when, after 1975, he became perhaps the least loved Conservative in the House of Commons, in the country at large he was rapidly being elevated into a 'Man for All Seasons'. It should also be noted that however much he may have been distressed by the progression of the Diehards after 1974, Mr Heath had himself articulated many similar sentiments on his own road to Downing Street after 1965. This gave a number of Conservatives (and Socialists) a sense of *déjà vu*,[1] and robbed the Ditcher cause of any sense of superiority which consistency brings to political debate.

As for Sir Keith Joseph, in the light of his unusual self effacement and his demonstrable compassion, it might have been agreeable to discover that his conversion to 'true' Conservatism in 1974 left him peerless amongst Conservatives and the recipient of universal felicitation. Coming as it did, however, in the wake of twenty years' acquiescence in and construction of something other than 'true' Conservatism, it is hardly surprising to find that this was not the case. His intellectual perspicacity had the misfortune to be combined with what proved to be, on occasion, a lack of political instinct. The result was that while he liked to refer to that 'certain diagnostic adventure' in his make-up,[2] others (not just Ditchers) called it lack of judgement. The immediate consequence was that while he was the object of much respect and even more wonderment, it could not be said that Sir Keith Joseph was entirely trusted. Mrs Thatcher was less brilliant and more astute. She was also more determined. Given her Diehard sentiments and ambitions, the salient feature about Mrs Thatcher is that once having become Conservative party leader she made few serious mistakes. By her own admission (see chapter 7, p.114) it might have been a mistake not to have participated more vigorously in the 1975 referendum campaign. It was also bad tactics to endorse the idea of a directly elected Scottish assembly (see chapter 7, p.116) so soon after becoming leader and so soon before withdrawing from the commitment. There were of course poor performances in the House of Commons, but these were soon forgotten, and in general, given her relative political inexperience, Mrs Thatcher acquitted herself with competence. The formula was simple. First, she listened to her own supporters, especially those in the House of Commons. Second, the fervent enunciation of Diehard views – she called herself a 'conviction politician' during the 1979 general election campaign[3] – was coupled with extreme caution in the area of explicit policy commitment. This combination was sometimes confusing, and perhaps a great mistake of the Labour party after 1975 was to dramatise Mrs Thatcher as hysterical and unreliable when they needed to appreciate that she was really a cautious political tactician with an eye to the main chance. In the nineteenth century, the Conservatives made the same mistake about Gladstone,[4] and he went on and on.

We will leave to the psephologists the problem of explaining *why* the Conservatives won the 1979 general election and conclude with the lesser task of assessing what happened to the Conservative party itself between losing office in February 1974 and regaining it in May 1979. A salient fact amidst the torrent of past events was the commencement (or more properly the re-commencement) of a debate in Conservative politics largely between Diehards and Ditchers about the nature of true Conservatism. Its chief participants were those who could be distinguished not so much by their different records of achievement and activity, but by their contrasting conceptions of the future. A major consequence of the debate itself was that after 1974 the Conservative party ceased to be the 'stupid' party. The chief protagonists rushed into print and the Conservative party (to the consternation of many) became intellectually respectable. It was no accident that hordes of disillusioned politicians, pamphleteers and academics, such as Mr Reg Prentice, Sir Richard Marsh, Mr Paul Johnson, Professor Hugh Thomas, Professor Max Beloff and Professor Alan Day, tumbled into the Conservative wheelbarrow. Like moths around a flickering candle, they hovered eagerly for a slice of the action. The surrender to the forces of intellect was not absolute. Indeed, 'common sense' continued to litter Conservative policy statements,[5] and it continued to inform industrial policy to the extent that Conservatives saw nothing untoward in orchestrating the depoliticisation of union activity from the bowels of Conservative Central Office. Nevertheless the march of reason was highlighted when the Conservative party was juxtaposed with a Labour party increasingly dominated after 1976 by someone who when he did not see himself as Moses appeared to many people to be taking lessons from Stanley Baldwin. This was Mr James Callaghan, a man 'of immense political experience and craftiness . . . effectively presenting himself to the nation as everybody's favourite uncle'. As Mr Peter Walker noted, the worry to the Conservatives was that 'Stanley Baldwin with the vote of the Labour Party and North Sea oil is a very formidable opponent'.[6]

The debate between Diehards and Ditchers was accompanied by personal antagonism and mutual recrimination and manifested itself physically with the removal of Mr Heath and his replacement by Mrs Thatcher in February 1975. What were the consequences of the Diehard leadership of Mrs Thatcher? First came the articulation of (Diehard) sentiments rooted in both liberal economics and deference for what were thought to be bourgeois values. This led the Conservative party down the path of less state activity, sound finance and emphasis

125

on personal responsibility. It released Conservative leaders, so they supposed, from the embarrassing problem of having to mount an intellectual defence of the confrontation with the miners in 1973. As Mrs Thatcher maintained (see chapter 5, p.73) this confrontation had been brought about by the state using an incomes policy to interfere in areas where it did not belong. When there was subsequent industrial unrest, in the winter of 1978, under a Labour Government also committed to incomes policy, Mrs Thatcher was triumphant. It did not matter that she was admonished by Mr Heath for gloating since she had positioned herself to say that it was incomes policies and not Conservative Governments which were a 'bad thing' and which caused confrontation. In short, the advantage of fighting the 1979 general election under a Diehard leader was that the question 'How will you deal with the unions?' could be answered fiercely 'We will deal with the unions in a different way from that which has twice engineered confrontation'.

Second, the Conservative leadership steered clear of making large numbers of detailed promises, and in a sense spent five years keeping its options open. The intention here was to win a general election and, unlike Mr Heath in 1970, be relatively free of encumbrances. The Conservative road to Downing Street was full of good intentions, but largely bereft of specific pledges. This circumspection put limits on the amount of change which took place after 1974. Beneath the fervent delineation of 'true' Conservatism, in the hard, black print of policy commitment, the closed shop, industrial intervention, the National Health Service, even incomes policy, were not proscribed. Change was limited by three further factors. First, the dispute between Diehards and Ditchers took place within limits. There was little disagreement between Conservatives about the importance of the rule of law, wealth and property and aspects of Conservative policy governed by these immutable glories changed hardly at all. Furthermore, there were large areas of policy — Europe, foreign affairs, decentralisation — which were not a stage for the Diehard-Ditcher battle. This did not mean that these subjects did not excite differences of opinion (these have not been focussed upon in our study) but, as we saw in chapter 7, these differences did not result in any fundamental shift away from strategies outlined by Mr Heath. In addition, like pugilists in a boxing ring Diehards and Ditchers had their own version of the Queensberry rules. There was general agreement within the party about the validity of the traditional form of Conservative conversation. Mrs Thatcher's leadership confirmed those aspects of the conversation used by Mr Heath (elitism in policy making and the distraction of local associations from expressly 'political' issues) and sponsored change only in so far as it led to the reassertion of the traditional form of conversation. Overall therefore, there was a substantial amount of continuity between 1974 and 1979.

What did the elevation of a Diehard leadership dominated by Sir Keith Joseph and Mrs Thatcher say about the esteem Conservatives held for the constitutional convention of collective cabinet responsibility and the idea of honour? It is very difficult to escape the conclusion that the short answer is that it did not say a great deal. In the words of Lord Salisbury (and according to Mrs Thatcher he was one of the best Prime Ministers we have ever had)[7] the convention of collective cabinet responsibility asserts that 'For all that passes in Cabinet each member of it who does not resign is absolutely and irretrievably responsible'.[8] No student of public administration would deny that there are difficulties for ministers carrying both individual departmental and collective cabinet responsibilities. Nor should he pretend that the exercise of judgement in politics would be a simple matter if only it were left to professional students of politics. Nevertheless, in the face of the turn-arounds of the Heath Government, only one politician of consequence and even then not a cabinet minister (Mr Teddy Taylor), saw fit to register his protest through the resignation of his office. How are we to react then, when within months (in some cases weeks) of losing office in 1974, leading members of the Heath administration were lining up to denounce it? Several reactions seem appropriate. First, to point out that when, in the wake of election defeat, politicians launch assaults on the decisions of a Government which were arrived at with their own approbation, they are very vulnerable to the charge that they spoke out only when they no longer had office to lose. Second, to point out that when, in addition, these same politicians invited the electorate to have confidence in their own competence, they should not have been surprised if questions were asked about their lack of judgement. Third, to point out that when these politicians articulated a set of (Diehard) principles which called upon individuals to stand upon their own two feet, it was not unreasonable to inquire, 'Where were you when the time came for *you* to stand up on your two feet?' And last, to point out that such apparent flouting of constitutional convention ill became a party which spent a good deal of time after 1974 thinking of ways to safeguard democratic government,[9] and accusing the Labour party of subverting the constitution.

To make these points is not, in this case, to aspire to the label Heathman or Powellite or constitutionalist. It is simply to reflect upon the interviewing of the most courteous of Conservative politicians who talked about their mere 'technical' responsibility for the actions of the Heath Government in which they served. It is the product of watching Conservative politicians denounce in opposition the very waste and bureaucracy which they themselves created in government. It is the result of reflection upon the activity of a party, the Conservative party, entrusting to leaders the task of shepherding the minions away from a history which those leaders had played a decisive part in creating.

Notes

1   Interview with Conservative MP, 27 October 1976.
2   Interview with shadow minister, 16 February 1978.
3   Thatcher, quoted in *The Guardian*, 17 April 1979.
4   Cooke and Vincent, *The Governing Passion*, 1974, p.66.
5   *The Right Approach*, 1976.
6   Maudling, open letter to constituents, *The Times*, 25 November 1977; Walker, quoted in *The Daily Telegraph*, 13 October 1977.
7   Thatcher, *The Sinews of Foreign Policy*, 1978, p.2.
8   Salisbury, quoted in Jennings, *Cabinet Government*, (1937), 1959, p.227.
9   Campbell (ed.), *Another Bill of Rights?*, 1976; Hailsham, *The Dilemma of Democracy*, 1978; Joseph, *Freedom Under the Law*, 1975.

Notes on sources

Interviews

A large number of conversations were held with Conservative politicians and officials. Only formal interviews, arranged by appointment, are listed below.

Conservative whip, House of Commons, 26 February 1976.
Conservative party vice-chairman, House of Commons, 26 February 1976.
Heath shadow minister, House of Commons, 8 June 1976.
Scottish Conservative MP, House of Commons, 20 October 1976.
Conservative MP, House of Commons, 27 October 1976.
Member of Thatcher's private office, London, 17 November 1976.
Heath shadow minister, London, 6 April 1977.
CTU national official, Central Office, 6 April 1977.
Conservative MP, House of Commons, 12 January 1978.
Thatcher shadow minister, House of Commons, 20 January 1978.
Conservative MP, House of Commons, 27 January 1978.
Thatcher shadow minister, House of Commons, 15 February 1978.
Thatcher shadow minister, House of Commons, 16 February 1978.
Department of Community Affairs official, Central Office, 25 September 1978.
Senior Central Office official, Central Office, 25 September 1978.
Prospective Conservative candidate, 20 October 1978; 26 April 1979.

Select bibliography

Beer, *Modern British Politics*, Faber & Faber, London, 1969 (1965).
Beloff, *Freedom Under Foot*, Maurice Temple Smith, London, 1976.
Berkeley, *Crossing the Floor*, Allen & Unwin, London, 1972.
Blake, *Disraeli*, Eyre & Spottiswode, London, 1966.
Blake, *The Conservative Party from Peel to Churchill*, Eyre & Spottiswode, London, 1970.
Blake and Patten (eds), *The Conservative Opportunity*, Macmillan, 1976.

Boyson (ed.), *1985: An Escape from Orwell's 1984*, Churchill, Enfield, 1975.

Boyson, *Centre Forward, a Radical Conservative Programme*, Temple Smith, London, 1978.

Buck (ed.), *How Conservatives Think*, Penguin, Harmondsworth, 1975.

Butler, *The Art of the Possible: the Memoirs of Lord Butler*, Penguin, Harmondsworth, 1973 (1971).

Butler, *The Tory Tradition, Bolingbroke—Burke, Disraeli—Salisbury*, John Murray, London, 1914.

Butler and Kavanagh, *The British General Election of February 1974*, Macmillan, London, 1974.

Butler and Kavanagh, *The British General Election of October 1974*, Macmillan, London, 1975.

Butler and Sloman (eds), *British Political Facts, 1900-75*, Macmillan, London, 1975.

Carr, *What is History?*, The George Macaulay Trevelyan Lectures delivered at the University of Cambridge, January-March 1961, Macmillan, London, 1972 (1961).

Cooke and Vincent, *The Governing Passion: Cabinet Government and Party Politics in Britain, 1885-6*, Harvester, Brighton, 1974.

Cosgrave, *Margaret Thatcher: a Tory and Her Party*, Hutchinson, London, 1978.

Dalyell, *Devolution: the End of Britain?*, Jonathan Cape, London, 1977.

Dangerfield, *The Strange Death of Liberal England*, Macgibbon & Key, London, 1961 (1935).

Disraeli, *Coningsby, or the New Generation*, Dent, London, 1967 (1844).

Disraeli, *Lord George Bentinck — a Political Biography*, Colborn, London, 1852.

Disraeli, *Sybil, or the Two Nations*, Oxford University Press (OUP), London, 1926 (1845).

Dowse and Hughes, *Political Sociology*, Wiley, London, 1972.

Dugdale, *Arthur James Balfour, First Earl of Balfour 1848-1905*, Hutchinson, London, 1939.

Fisher, *The Tory Leaders: Their Struggle for Power*, Weidenfeld & Nicolson, London, 1977.

Gamble, *The Conservative Nation*, Routledge & Kegan Paul, London, 1974.

Gardiner, *Margaret Thatcher from Childhood to Leadership*, Kimber, London, 1975.

Gilmour, *Insight Right, a Study of Conservatism*, Hutchinson, London, 1977.

Hailsham, *The Dilemma of Democracy: Diagnosis and Prescription*, Collins, London, 1978.

Hailsham, *The Door Wherein I Went*, Collins, London, 1975.

Hayek, *The Constitution of Liberty*, Routledge & Kegan Paul, London, 1960.

Hayek, *The Road to Serfdom*, Routledge & Kegan Paul, London, 1976 (1944).

Hurd, *An End to Promises: Sketch of a Government 1970-74*, Collins, London, 1979.

Hutchinson, *Edward Heath — a Personal and Political Biography*, Longman, London, 1978.

Jennings, *Cabinet Government*, Cambridge University Press, Cambridge, 1959 (1937).

Joseph, *Reversing the Trend*, Barry Rose, London, 1975.

Joseph, *Stranded on the Middle Ground?*, Centre for Policy Studies, London, 1976.

Kilmuir, *Political Adventure: the Memoirs of the Earl of Kilmuir*, Weidenfeld & Nicolson, London, 1964.

King, *The Cecil King Diary, 1965-70*, Jonathan Cape, London, 1972.

Lewis, *Margaret Thatcher — a Personal and Political Biography*, Routledge & Kegan Paul, London, 1975.

Lindsay and Harrington, *The Conservative Party 1918-70*, Macmillan, London, 1974.

Longford, *Wellington: Pillar of State*, Weidenfeld & Nicolson, London, 1975 (1972).

Maudling, *Memoirs*, Sidgwick & Jackson, London, 1978.

McKenzie, *British Political Parties*, Heinemann, London, 1964 (1955).

Money, *First Lady in the House*, Frewin, 1975.

Monypenny and Buckle, *The Life of Benjamin Disraeli*, John Murray, London, 1912-20.

Murray, *Margaret Thatcher*, Allen, London, 1978.

Oakeshott, *Rationalism in Politics*, Methuen, London, 1962.

Powell, *Wrestling with the Angel*, Sheldon, London, 1977.

Punnett, *Front Bench Opposition*, Heinemann, London, 1973.

Raison, *Why Conservative?*, Penguin, Harmondsworth, 1964.

Ritchie (ed.), *Enoch Powell: a Nation or No Nation, Six Years in British Politics*, Batsford, London, 1978.

Rogaly, *Grunwick*, Penguin, Harmondsworth, 1977.

Rose, *The Problem of Party Government*, Macmillan, London, 1974.

Roth, *Heath and the Heathmen*, Routledge & Kegan Paul, London, 1972.

Russel, *The Tory Party*, Penguin, Harmondswoth, 1978.

Sampson, *Macmillan: a Study in Ambiguity*, Penguin, Harmondsworth, 1968 (1967).

Waldegrave, *The Binding of Leviathan, Conservatism and the Future*, Hamish Hamilton, London, 1978.

Walker, *The Ascent of Britain*, Sidgwick & Jackson, London, 1977.

Ward, *Fort Grunwick*, Temple Smith, London, 1977.

Watkins (ed.), *In Defence of Freedom*, Cassell, London, 1978.

Young, *Victorian England: Portrait of an Age*, Oxford Paperback, London, 1969 (1936).

Articles and pamphlets

Behrens, 'Blinkers for the carthorse: the Conservative party and the trade unions, 1974-78', *The Political Quarterly*, 1978.

Behrens, 'Diehards and Ditchers in contemporary Conservative politics', *The Political Quarterly*, 1979.

Behrens, *The Conservative Party in Opposition 1974-77 — a Critical Analysis*, Lanchester Polytechnic Monograph, 1977.

Benedictus, 'Employment protection: new institutions and trade union rights', *Industrial Law Journal*, 1976.

Blake, *Conservatism in an Age of Revolution*, Churchill, London, 1976.

Bulpitt, 'English law politics: the collapse of the ancien régime', *Political Studies Association Conference Paper*, 1976.

Carr, 'Incomes policy', *The Political Quarterly*, 1975.

Cosgrave, 'Heath as Prime Minister', *The Political Quarterly*, 1973.

Drake, 'Recent legislation: old wine in new bottles', *Industrial Law Journal*, 1974.

Drake, 'The Trade Union and Labour Relations Act 1974', *Modern Law Review*, 1974.

Drake, 'The Trade Union and Labour Relations (Amendment) Bill', *Industrial Law Journal*, 1976.

Glickman, 'The Toryness of English Conservatism', *Journal of British Studies*, 1962.

Jordan, 'The committee stage of the Scotland and Wales Bill, (1976-77)', *The Waverley Papers*, occasional paper 1, 1979.

Layton-Henry, 'Constituency authority in the Conservative party', *Parliamentary Affairs*, 1976.

Pinto-Duschinsky, 'Central Office and power in the Conservative party', *Political Studies*, 1972.

Raison, 'The state of Conservatism', *The Round Table*, 1977.

Seyd, 'Case study: democracy within the Conservative party?', *Government and Opposition*, 1975.

Stanyer, 'Irresistible forces: the pressures for a science of politics', *Political Studies*, 1976.

Stanyer, 'Nationalism, regionalism, and the British system of government', *Social and Economic Administration*, 1974.

Weekes, 'Law and the practice of the closed shop', *Industrial Law Journal*, 1976.

Wilson, 'Constituency party autonomy and central control', *Political Studies*, 1973.

Miscellaneous

Newspapers and periodicals

The Daily Mail, 1974-79
The Daily Telegraph, 1974-79
The Financial Times, 1974-79
The Guardian, 1974-79
The Sun, 1975
The Sunday Express, 1974-79
The Sunday Times, 1974-78
The Times, 1974-78

The Bradford Telegraph and Argus, 1978
The Brighton Reformer, 1976
The Manchester Evening News, 1974-79
Campaign, 1977-79
Conservative Monthly News, later *Conservative News*, 1974-79
Crossbow, the journal of the Bow Group, 1973-79
Free Nation, the fortnightly paper of the National Association for Freedom 1976-9
Labour Research, 1973-79
New Society, 1972
Small Business, 1977-78
The Cambridge Reformer, the research magazine of the Cambridge Tory Reform Group, 1977
The Conservative Agent's Journal (for private circulation to members only)
The Illustrated London News, 1976
The New Statesman, 1974-79
The Socialist Commentary, 1974-78
The Spectator, 1974-79
Tory Challenge, Monday Club journal, 1977
Westminster Confidential, 1976-77
Woman's Own, 1976

Selected Conservative Political Centre publications

Alison, Baker, Brittan, Butler, Goodhart (eds), *One Nation at Work*, 1976.

Biffen, *A Nation in Doubt*, 1976.

Campbell et al., *Another Bill of Rights?*, 1976.

CPC/Monthly Report, 1974-75.

Du Cann, *Parliament and the Purse Strings: How to Bring Public Expenditure Under Parliamentary Control*, 1977.

Griffiths, *Fighting for the Life of Freedom*, 1977.

Hailsham, *The Acceptable Face of Western Civilisation*, 1973.

Heath, *Our Community*, 1977.

Holland and Fallon, *The Quango Explosion: Public Bodies and Ministerial Patronage*, 1978.

Howell, *Time to Move On*, 1976.

Royle (ed.), *Our Voice in Europe*, 1976.

Tugendhat, *Britain, Europe and the Third World*, 1976.

Tugendhat, *Conservatives in Europe*, 1979.

Selected Conservative Central Office publications

A Better Tomorrow: the Conservative Programme for the Next Five Years, 1970.

A Strategy for Union Members, Conservative Trade Unionists, 1978.

Central Council Meeting Handbook, the National Union of Conservative and Unionist Associations, 1977.

Conservative Trade Unionists (CTU) News, 1978.

The Conservative and Unionist Central Office Annual Reports, 1975-76, 1976-77, 1977-78.

Maude (ed.), *The Right Approach to the Economy, Outline of an Economic Strategy for the Next Conservative Government*, 1977.

News Service, 1974-79.

Putting Britain First: a National Policy from the Conservatives, 1974.

Procedure for the Selection of the Leader of the Conservative Party, 1974.

The Campaign Guide, 1974.

The Campaign Guide, 1977.

The Conservative Manifesto, 1979.

Income and Expenditure Account of the Central Funds of the Conservative and Unionist Party for years ended 31 March 1971-1975.

The 93rd Conservative Conference Handbook, 1976.

The 94th Conservative Conference Handbook, 1977.

The 95th Conservative Conference Handbook, 1978.

The Right Approach, a Statement of Conservative Aims, 1976.

Trade Union News, 1978.

Others

Hansard, 1974-79.

The House of Commons Official Report, 1974-78.

The Report of a Court of Inquiry under the Rt Hon. Lord Justice Scarman OBE into a Dispute between Grunwick Processing Laboratories Limited and Members of the Association of Professional, Executive, Clerical and Computer Staff, Cmnd 6922, August 1977.

Biffen, *Political Office or Political Power?, Six Speeches on National and International Affairs*, Centre for Policy Studies, 1977.

Conservative Conference Verbatim Reports, 1970-78.

Conservative Trade Unionists' Annual Conference Handbook, Bradford, 1978.

Daily Notes, Conservative Research Department, 1979.

Jackson (ed.), *Conservatives in Europe*, European Conservative Group, 1979.

Joseph, *Monetarism is Not Enough*, Centre for Policy Studies, 1976.

Joseph, *The Business of Business*, Bow Group, 1977.

Labour Party Research Department, *Information Papers*, 1974-78.

Lyon and Wigram, *Electoral Reform: the House of Lords*, Conservative Action for Electoral Reform, 1977.

Margaret Thatcher in North America. Extracts from the Leader's Speeches in New York, Washington, Chicago, Toronto, N.D.

Ridley, *Social Service Sense*, Bow Group, 1977.

Rippon, *Our European Future*, European Conservative Group, N.D.

Thatcher, *Europe as I See it*, European Conservative Group, 1977.

Thatcher, Howe, Joseph, *The Right Angle, Three Studies in Conservatism*, Bow Group, 1979.

Thatcher, *The Sinews of Foreign Policy*, European Conservative Group, 1978.

The William Wilson Papers, Modern Records Centre, University of Warwick Library.

Index

Ridley, Nicholas, 70, 72
Rifkind, Malcolm, 116
Rippon, Sir Geoffrey, 62
Rodgers, Sir John, 30
Rolls Royce, 34, 56
Rowe, Andrew, 51-2

Saatchi and Saatchi Garland-Compton, 58, 59, 123
Scarman, Lord, 96, 97
Scarman Report, 79, 96-7
Skinner, Dennis, 106
Scott, Nicholas, 62, 73, 107, 118
Scottish Development Agency 109
Selsdon Group, 8, 59, 94, 97
Shelton, William, 39
Sherman, Alfred, 62
Silkin, John, 92
Silvester, Fred, 48
Soames, Sir Christopher, 37
Speed, Keith, 112
Steel, David, 28

Taylor, Edward, 10, 62, 107, 110, 113, 116-7, 127
Taylor, Sir John, 50
Tebbit, Norman, 62, 94
Thatcher, Margaret, 2, 9, 10, 15; housing policy 27; 1975 leadership contest 38-41, 47, 48-50, 52; publicity 57-9; speeches 62-3; leadership style 63-4, 72, 77, 79; union reform 79-80, 82-3; trade unions 87, 92, 98, 99, 103; immigration 104-5, 111; defence 113; Europe 114; China 114-5; Ireland 115-6;

devolution 116-8; immigration 118-9, 123, 124-5, 126-7
Thomas, Professor Hugh, 125
Thomas, Peter, 33, 62
Thorneycroft, Lord, 52-4, 64-5
Thorpe, Jeremy, 28, 56
Tilney, Lady, 57
Tory Reform Group, 59, 73, 97, 107
Trade Union and Labour Relations Act 1974, 89, 90, 91
Trade Union and Labour Relations (Amendment) Act 1976, 89, 90, 91, 93
Trade Union Congress, 77, 88, 90, 93
Tugenhat, 114

Ulster Unionists, 115
Union of Post Office Workers (UPW), 95
Upper Clyde Shipyards, 35
Utley, T.E., 62

Waldegrave, William, 12
Walker, Peter, 13, 40, 60, 62, 73, 74, 107, 118, 125
Ward, George, 96, 97
Webster, Sir Richard, 64
Welsh Development Agency, 109
Whitelaw, William, 2, 16, 31, 37, 38, 40, 41, 59, 63, 111, 116, 119
Wilson, Sir Harold, 18, 24
Williams, Shirley, 59
Winterton, Nicholas, 28
Wood, Richard, 37
Wolff, Michael, 33, 64